LEGAL DECISION-MAKING UNDER THE NATIONAL VOCATIONAL EDUCATION AND TRAINING REGULATOR ACT 2011 (CTH):

AN INVESTIGATION INTO ACCESS TO MERITS REVIEW

Ms Raelene Bartlett

LEGAL DECISION-MAKING UNDER THE NATIONAL VOCATIONAL EDUCATION AND TRAINING REGULATOR ACT 2011 (CTH): AN INVESTIGATION INTO ACCESS TO MERITS REVIEW

Get 15 minutes **OBLIGATION FREE** Consultation with Raelene:
https://rtodoctor.com.au/contact/

Join the Facebook group '**RTO Doctor**' for FREE tips, resources, videos and more.

See the back page of this book for your SPECIAL DISCOUNT OFFERS

Author: Raelene Bartlett
Title: Legal Decision-Making Under the National Vocational Education and Training Regulator Act 2011 (Cth):
Subtitle: An Investigation into Merits Review
Subjects: Administrative Law; Regulatory Practice; Commonwealth Legislation; Administrative Appeals Tribunal; Merits review; Judicial Review; Education; International Education; Education Services for Overseas Students (ESOS); Regulation; Compliance; Registered Training Organisations (RTOs); Australian Skills Quality Authority; ASQA.

LEGAL DECISION-MAKING UNDER THE NATIONAL VOCATIONAL EDUCATION AND TRAINING REGULATOR ACT 2011 (CTH): AN INVESTIGATION INTO ACCESS TO MERITS REVIEW

For all enquiries, contact Raelene at
https://rtodoctor.com.au/contact/

LEGAL DECISION-MAKING UNDER THE NATIONAL VOCATIONAL EDUCATION AND TRAINING REGULATOR ACT 2011 (CTH): AN INVESTIGATION INTO ACCESS TO MERITS REVIEW

LEGAL DECISION-MAKING UNDER THE NATIONAL VOCATIONAL EDUCATION AND TRAINING REGULATOR ACT 2011 (CTH): AN INVESTIGATION INTO ACCESS TO MERITS REVIEW

LEGAL DECISION-MAKING UNDER THE NATIONAL VOCATIONAL EDUCATION AND TRAINING REGULATOR ACT 2011 (CTH): AN INVESTIGATION INTO ACCESS TO MERITS REVIEW

Introduction

Overview

This paper discusses the legal decision-making process as it applies to the *National Vocational Education and Training Regulator Act 2011* (Cth) ("NVR Act") and how this impacts access to merits review while highlighting some significant areas of concern. These areas of concern are a cause for alarm at the highest levels of government and the judiciary.

This paper does not seek to offer solutions. This paper was initially prepared[1] in partial completion of a Supervised Legal Research project in the Faculty of Law at Murdoch University in Western Australia as part of a

---

[1] This paper has been slightly amended and expanded since it was submitted as a Supervised Legal Research project. Amendments include new cases that had been released on AustLii, the inclusion of findings from the Callinan review of the AAT (n 61) and lecturer feedback.

LEGAL DECISION-MAKING UNDER THE NATIONAL VOCATIONAL EDUCATION AND TRAINING REGULATOR ACT 2011 (CTH): AN INVESTIGATION INTO ACCESS TO MERITS REVIEW

Bachelor of Laws (Graduate Entry). It merely seeks to highlight these areas of concern to enable focussed and critical discussions and investigations to commence. It is also hoped that this paper will be the basis for further research.

Some of the key topics that will be discussed include consideration of issues of public interest and the concerns that are raised when the very basis for legal decisions under the NVR Act is potentially flawed and based on an unqualified foundation. The research considers the legal meaning and interpretation of the term *'decision'* looking to statute and case law for guidance; a crucial factor for this research because if an administrative action (such as those referred to in this paper) does not constitute a *'decision'* for the purposes of the *Administrative Decisions (Judicial Review) Act 1997* (Cth), it cannot be reviewed.

LEGAL DECISION-MAKING UNDER THE NATIONAL VOCATIONAL EDUCATION AND TRAINING REGULATOR ACT 2011 (CTH): AN INVESTIGATION INTO ACCESS TO MERITS REVIEW

While reviewing *Australian Broadcasting Tribunal v Bond*,[2] suggests that the steps in the process of making a final determination do not, in themselves form the final decision, it is precisely on the basis of these 'steps' that decisions are being made by the Australian Skills Quality Authority ("ASQA"). This paper highlights that the reasons given by ASQA in their legal decisions explicitly state that the *'decision'* has been made due to non-compliance with the legislative requirements that these 'steps' are based upon.

Another key area of focus in this paper is that of the Model Litigant Obligation in the *Legal Services Directions 2017* (Cth) and how adherence to this *'Obligation'* by ASQA lawyers as model litigants continues to be a cause for concern amongst legal practitioners.

---

2 *Australian Broadcasting Tribunal v Bond* [1990] HCA 33

LEGAL DECISION-MAKING UNDER THE NATIONAL VOCATIONAL EDUCATION AND TRAINING REGULATOR ACT 2011 (CTH): AN INVESTIGATION INTO ACCESS TO MERITS REVIEW

Introduction to the regulatory ambition of Vocational Education and Training (VET) and International Education (IE) in Australia

Australia's VET/IE system is significant, complex and an important contributor to Australia's economy. However, Bowman and McKenna[3] report that:

> Twenty years after the introduction of a national training system, it is still difficult to find a consistent statement about its purpose, objectives and key elements.

It should come as no surprise then that the regulatory ambition of the VET/IE sector in Australia is just as complex.

The regulation of Australia's VET/IE sectors has historically been a shared responsibility between the

---

[3] Kay Bowman and Suzy McKenna, *The Development of Australia's National Training System: A Dynamic Tension Between Consistency and Flexibility* (NCVER, 2016) 16 [2].

LEGAL DECISION-MAKING UNDER THE NATIONAL VOCATIONAL EDUCATION AND TRAINING REGULATOR ACT 2011 (CTH): AN INVESTIGATION INTO ACCESS TO MERITS REVIEW

Commonwealth, the States and Territories. On 1 July 2011, a national regulator, the ASQA was established under the NVR Act; it shares this responsibility with the Training and Accreditation Council ("TAC") in Western Australia and the Victorian Registration and Qualifications Authority ("VRQA") in Victoria. This is further complicated by the State and Territory governments who provide funding to certain providers and may also, under a Memorandum of Understanding, share regulatory responsibility with the national regulator via delegation. These delegated arrangements are noted in the schools' sector (primary and secondary schools across Australia and certain public providers, specifically Technical and Further Education ("TAFE") colleges.

Adding further complexity, ASQA also shares its regulatory functions with the Tertiary Education and Quality Standards Agency ("TEQSA") for all

LEGAL DECISION-MAKING UNDER THE NATIONAL VOCATIONAL EDUCATION AND TRAINING REGULATOR ACT 2011 (CTH): AN INVESTIGATION INTO ACCESS TO MERITS REVIEW

organisations, public or private, who provide higher qualifications in Australia.

While higher education includes qualifications under the Australian Qualifications Framework ("AQF") between AQF levels 5 and 10, some of these qualifications are also delivered in the VET sector. TEQSA is the ESOS Agency[4] for the purposes of the *Education Services for Overseas Students Act 2000* (Cth) ("ESOS Act") for ELICOS[5] and Foundation Programs[6] providers.

The Council of Australian Government ("COAG") Industry Skills Council ("CISC") has overall responsibility for industry competitiveness, productivity, labour market pressures, skills development and national

---

[4] *Education Services for Overseas Students Act 2000* (Cth) s 5.
[5] ELICOS - English Language Intensive Courses for Overseas Students.
[6] Foundation Programs courses are those courses defined by the legislative instrument *Education Services for Overseas Students 2000 - Foundation Program Standards.*

11

LEGAL DECISION-MAKING UNDER THE
NATIONAL VOCATIONAL EDUCATION AND
TRAINING REGULATOR ACT 2011 (CTH): AN
INVESTIGATION INTO ACCESS TO MERITS
REVIEW

training arrangements. The Australian Industry Skills Committee ("AISC") was established in May 2015 after the National Skills Standards Council ("NSSC"), established in July 2011 (which replaced the National Quality Council) was disbanded.

Since Australia has endeavoured to formalise the national framework underpinning the VET sector, it has seen many changes. Those changes appear to occur in a cyclic manner with the fundamental premise to provide a national system that encourages quality and compliance with a set of *'Quality Standards'*.[7]

In that context, *'someone'* needed to monitor compliance with those Standards, and this has inevitably resulted in this shared responsibility between the Commonwealth, States and Territories. On 1 July 2011, the VET/IE

---

[7] *National Vocational Education and Training Regulator Act 2011* (Cth) s 231A

LEGAL DECISION-MAKING UNDER THE NATIONAL VOCATIONAL EDUCATION AND TRAINING REGULATOR ACT 2011 (CTH): AN INVESTIGATION INTO ACCESS TO MERITS REVIEW

landscape changed immeasurably with the introduction of the NVR Act and the VET Quality Framework ("VQF")[8].

COAG's intention for ASQA was to maximise efficiency and facilitate greater consistency of regulation'.[9] The situation is best described in the following diagram:[10]

---

[8] The VQF includes the *Standards for Registered Training Organisations (RTOs) 2015* (Cth) ("Standards for RTOs"), the *Fit and Proper Persons Requirements 2011* (Cth) ("FPP Requirements"), the *Financial Viability Risk Assessment Requirements 2011* (Cth) ("FVRAR"), the *Data Collection Requirements 2012* (Cth) ("DCR") and the Australian Qualifications Framework (2nd Edition) ("AQF").

[9] Valerie Braithwaite, *All Eyes on Quality: Review of the National Vocational Education and Training Regulator Act 2011 Report* (January 2018).

[10] Bowman and McKenna (n 3).

LEGAL DECISION-MAKING UNDER THE NATIONAL VOCATIONAL EDUCATION AND TRAINING REGULATOR ACT 2011 (CTH): AN INVESTIGATION INTO ACCESS TO MERITS REVIEW

Figure 1   National frameworks for VET products and providers initiatives since the late 1980s

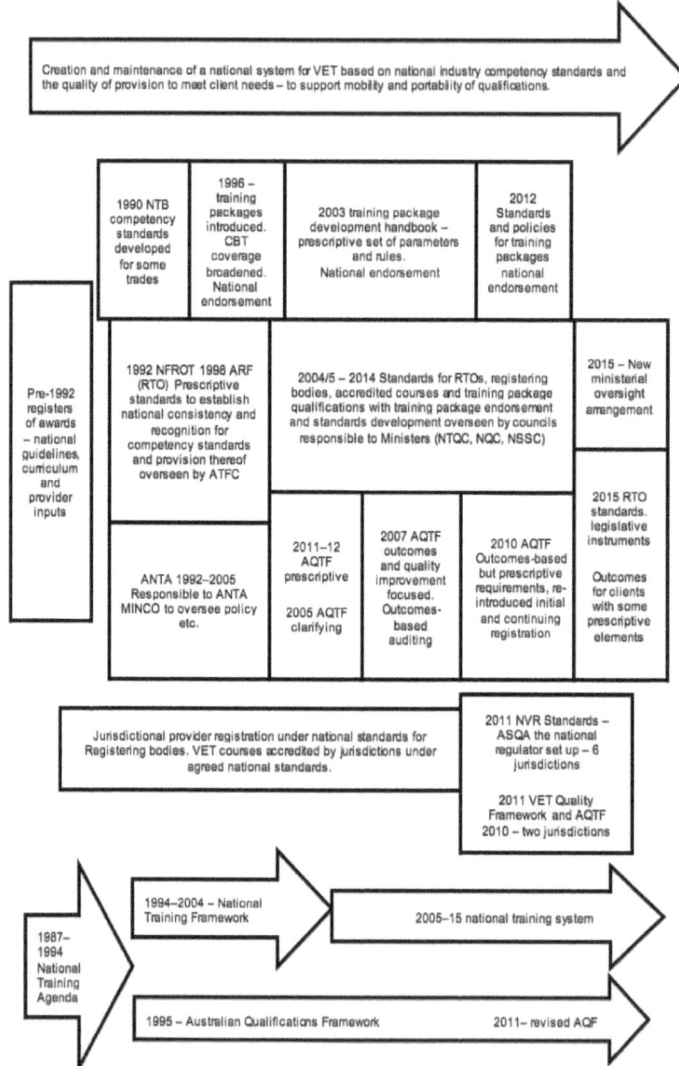

Notes: NTB = National Training Board; NFROT = National Framework for the Recognition of Training; ARF = Australian Recognition Framework; ATFC = Australian Training Framework Committee; MINCO = Ministerial Council; AQTF = Australian Quality Training Framework; ASQA = Australian Skills Quality Authority; NTQ = National Training Council; NQC = National Quality Council; NSSC = National Skills Standards Council.

LEGAL DECISION-MAKING UNDER THE NATIONAL VOCATIONAL EDUCATION AND TRAINING REGULATOR ACT 2011 (CTH): AN INVESTIGATION INTO ACCESS TO MERITS REVIEW

ASQA is responsible for regulating all Registered Training Organisations ("RTOs") nationally.[11]

Braithwaite[12] found:

> As of November 2017, ASQA was responsible for regulating 4,061 RTOs, while Victoria and Western Australia, who have not referred their powers, regulate 242 and 235 respectively.

These numbers are in a constant state of flux due to a range of factors including those considered by this research.

This research is focussed on ASQA and its appeals process which includes the Administrative Appeals Tribunal ("AAT"), specifically, legal decision-making and access to merits review by ASQA regulated training

---

[11] With the exception of two (2) jurisdictions under limited circumstances TAC and VRQA refused to hand over their powers to the Commonwealth and these regulators both operate independently of ASQA.

[12] Braithwaite (n 9) 13 [4].

providers focussing on 'stay' decisions. TAC and the VRQA operate under very different appeals processes, therefore will not be considered by this paper.[13]

---

[13] There are limited circumstances where providers that are registered in either Western Australia or Victoria cannot maintain registration under their respective State regulators. These include where the provider is registered on the Commonwealth Register of Institutions and Courses for Overseas Students (CRICOS), where they are delivering nationally recognised training online or in an ASQA regulated jurisdiction and where they are providing ELICOS.

LEGAL DECISION-MAKING UNDER THE NATIONAL VOCATIONAL EDUCATION AND TRAINING REGULATOR ACT 2011 (CTH): AN INVESTIGATION INTO ACCESS TO MERITS REVIEW

Size of the VET/IE sector in Australia

In its March 2019 statistics, the Commonwealth[14] confirmed:

> Australian international education, as well as being one of Australia's largest export industries and contributing nearly $35 billion to the Australian economy in 2018, is also a significant creator of jobs in Australia.

This is an increase from the Department's figures in 2017 showing that international education contributed $30.8 billion to the Australian economy with 27% of those enrolments in the VET sector.

It is important to recognise however that there is often much cross-over between the different sectors (Schools,

---

[14] Department of Education and Training (DET) 'Jobs supported by international students studying in Australia' (Research Snapshots, March 2019) <https://internationaleducation.gov.au/research/Research-Snapshots/Documents/RS_Job%20supported%202018.pdf>.

LEGAL DECISION-MAKING UNDER THE NATIONAL VOCATIONAL EDUCATION AND TRAINING REGULATOR ACT 2011 (CTH): AN INVESTIGATION INTO ACCESS TO MERITS REVIEW

VET, Higher Education and ELICOS) and in many cases, students will often follow an integrated pathway or package. A common example of such a package might be that the student arrives and completes 12 weeks of English language study with an ELICOS provider. They then complete a Certificate III, Certificate IV, Diploma and Advanced Diploma with an RTO then finish their study in Australia with a bachelor's degree at University.

Advice to Parliament about the size of Australia's VET sector outside the international education market in November 2018 included:

> In 2017, an estimated 4.2 million students were enrolled in VET with an Australian training provider, representing almost a quarter of the Australian population aged 15–64 years. In comparison, in the same year, there were 1.5 million higher education students enrolled with

LEGAL DECISION-MAKING UNDER THE NATIONAL VOCATIONAL EDUCATION AND TRAINING REGULATOR ACT 2011 (CTH): AN INVESTIGATION INTO ACCESS TO MERITS REVIEW

an Australian higher education provider, and 3.8 million school students enrolled in Australia...The majority of students (60.2%) were enrolled with a private training provider only, while the next largest group were enrolled with a TAFE institution only (16.1%).[15]

This helps demonstrate why the VET/IE sector is constantly under the spotlight in the media and is often used as a political handball.

The VET/IE system in Australia is a complex web, partly due to non-harmonised jurisdictions in the attempt by COAG[16] referred to earlier to develop

---

[15] Joint Standing Committee on Migration, Parliament of Australia, *Report of the Inquiry into Efficacy of Current Regulation of Australian Migration and Education Agents* (February 2019) <https://www.aph.gov.au/Parliamentary_Business/Committees/Joint /Migration/Migrationagentregulatio/Report>.

LEGAL DECISION-MAKING UNDER THE NATIONAL VOCATIONAL EDUCATION AND TRAINING REGULATOR ACT 2011 (CTH): AN INVESTIGATION INTO ACCESS TO MERITS REVIEW

uniform, national regulation of the sector while integrating components of the General Skilled Migration ("GSM") program and the ELICOS sector.

Further complicating this regulatory framework is that some of these programs are offered across primary and secondary schools, both government and private schools as well as the TAFE and University sector, including Non-Self-Accrediting Institutions ("NSAI's") operating in the University space.[17]

The regulation of the VET/IE sector is perhaps so complex because it lacks clarity in what it is trying to

---

[16] Council of Australian Governments, *'Council of Australian Governments' Meeting Communiqué'*, (February 2009) 5 [2].

[17] While technically, Technical and Further Education ("TAFE") institutions are classified as Registered Training Organisations (RTOs), they are often not recognised as such by the public and media. There is evidence (see Bibliography reference to The Hon Simon Birmingham) that they are not regulated in the same manner as 'traditional' RTOs and receive preferential treatment due to their status as government entities. Under this umbrella of complex regulatory oversight, is further regulation by State and/or Territory funding bodies and delegated powers of regulation to State/Territory regulators for certain education and training providers.

LEGAL DECISION-MAKING UNDER THE NATIONAL VOCATIONAL EDUCATION AND TRAINING REGULATOR ACT 2011 (CTH): AN INVESTIGATION INTO ACCESS TO MERITS REVIEW

achieve, as well as the often-interchanging political portfolios that it tends to fall into. Internationally known as Technical Vocational Education and Training ("TVET"), Todd and Dunbar on behalf of UNESCO[18] state:

> TVET cuts across every sector of the economy, and relies on effective dialogue and interaction between education and training providers, labour market stakeholders including employers, worker representatives, and other stakeholders. In addition TVET is expected to contribute towards a wide range of (sometimes contradictory) socioeconomic goals, including full employment, increased productivity and competitiveness, social cohesion, equity and sustainability...Given this context it is no surprise that governments have experienced difficulty in formulating,

---

[18] Robin Todd and Muriel Dunbar, UNESCO, 'Taking A Whole of Government Approach to Skills Development' (2018) 14 [1.1:2].

LEGAL DECISION-MAKING UNDER THE NATIONAL VOCATIONAL EDUCATION AND TRAINING REGULATOR ACT 2011 (CTH): AN INVESTIGATION INTO ACCESS TO MERITS REVIEW

planning, managing, implementing and evaluating effective TVET and skills development policies, strategies and plans.

LEGAL DECISION-MAKING UNDER THE NATIONAL VOCATIONAL EDUCATION AND TRAINING REGULATOR ACT 2011 (CTH): AN INVESTIGATION INTO ACCESS TO MERITS REVIEW

ASQA – Its Role and Operation

In its review of ASQA's operations and processes, Pricewaterhouse Coopers ("PwC") found that 'Given ASQA's position as a national VET regulator, PwC could not identify any directly comparable regulatory organisations against which to assess ASQA'.[19] While some might argue that TEQSA is a comparable regulator, in terms of numbers of providers regulated and the self-accrediting nature of the majority of its providers, TEQSA's regulatory model is quite dissimilar.[20]

ASQA is an independent statutory agency meaning that a delegate exercises powers under the relevant legislation independently although the Minister remains accountable for the decision.[21] It performs a number of

---

[19] Pricewaterhouse Coopers, '*ASQA Process Review: Final Report*' (2013) [10].

[20] Tertiary Education Standards Agency, '*What Approach to Quality Assurance and Regulation*' (Web Page) <https://www.teqsa.gov.au/what-we-do>.

[21] Judith Bannister, Anna Olijnyk and Stephen McDonald,

LEGAL DECISION-MAKING UNDER THE NATIONAL VOCATIONAL EDUCATION AND TRAINING REGULATOR ACT 2011 (CTH): AN INVESTIGATION INTO ACCESS TO MERITS REVIEW

roles while operating on a full cost-recovery basis. ASQA's independence as a national regulator[22] means that it is not subject to direction from anyone in relation to the performance of its functions or the exercise of its powers.

The Chief Commissioner of ASQA is delegated power from the Minister[23] to make those decisions to which this research relates while the NVR Regulator is authorised to delegate their power to a range of people and bodies that make up government authorities,[24] occupational licensing and other bodies[25] and to certain self-regulating RTOs.[26] This provides the foundation for legal decision-making under the NVR Act.

Government *Accountability - Australian Administrative Law,* (Cambridge University Press NS, 2nd Edition, 2018).

[22] *National Vocational Education and Training Regulator Act 2011* (Cth) s 259.

[23] Ibid s 223.

[24] Ibid s 224.

[25] Ibid s 225.

[26] Ibid s 226.

LEGAL DECISION-MAKING UNDER THE NATIONAL VOCATIONAL EDUCATION AND TRAINING REGULATOR ACT 2011 (CTH): AN INVESTIGATION INTO ACCESS TO MERITS REVIEW

ASQA has four (4) main responsibilities under the NVR Act being:

- Registration of training providers and courses under the NVR Act;[27]
- Manage changes to registration and courses;
- Ensuring compliance with the VQF;
- Accreditation of courses.

ASQA exerts its ESOS Agency responsibilities below[28] concurrent with its responsibilities under the NVR Act where relevant.

Findings are usually determined under the NVR Act first and either eliminated or further assessed against the

---

[27] Training providers and courses are registered separately under the NVR Act however a course cannot be registered if the provider is not registered.

[28] It should be noted that a provider cannot be registered under the ESOS Act for VET courses if it is not registered as an RTO first, albeit, some applications are reviewed concurrently (*Education Services for Overseas Students Act 2000* (Cth), s 6E(1)(b).

LEGAL DECISION-MAKING UNDER THE NATIONAL VOCATIONAL EDUCATION AND TRAINING REGULATOR ACT 2011 (CTH): AN INVESTIGATION INTO ACCESS TO MERITS REVIEW

ESOS Act requirements subsequent to the initial findings including:

- Registration of training providers and courses;[29]

- Manage changes to registration and courses;

- Ensure compliance with the ESOS Act and National Code;[30]

- Undertake enforcement action against providers who do not comply with the Act or legislative instruments made under the Act.

ASQA's legal representatives often refer to, and rely upon their responsibilities in fulfilling the objectives of the NVR Act as one of the key reasons why a stay decision should not be granted prior to a review decision

---

[29] Training providers and courses are registered separately under the ESOS Act however a course cannot be registered if the provider is not registered.

[30] The *National Code of Practice for Providers of Education and Training to Overseas Students 2018* ("National Code") is a legislative instrument made under s 33 of the ESOS Act.

LEGAL DECISION-MAKING UNDER THE NATIONAL VOCATIONAL EDUCATION AND TRAINING REGULATOR ACT 2011 (CTH): AN INVESTIGATION INTO ACCESS TO MERITS REVIEW

taking place by the Tribunal.[31] ASQA lawyers appear to have less need recently to reinforce these responsibilities at the outset or in their Statements of Issues, Facts and Contentions as it would appear that it is not uncommon now for Tribunal members to identify ASQA's responsibilities without any provocation in its decision-making.[32] It would ordinarily be expected that ASQA lawyers would point toward these responsibilities and spell them out more explicitly when defending their

---

[31] *VETiS Consulting Services Pty Ltd ('VETiS') v Australian Skills Quality Authority* [2019] AATA 341 (7 March 2019) [5], *Institute of Training Pty Ltd ('Institute of Technical Training') v Australian Skills Quality Authority* [2018] AATA 4127 (5 November 2018) [39], *Technical Education Australia Pty Ltd ('Technical Education Australia') v Australian Skills Quality Authority* [2018] AATA 3047 (23 August 2018) [104 - 105], *Trades College Australia Pty Ltd ('Trades College Australia') v Australian Skills Quality Authority* [2018] AATA 1703 (12 June 2018) [16], *Australian Institute of Technical Training Pty Ltd ('Australian Institute') v Australian Skills Quality Authority* [2018] AATA 1281 (11 May 2018) [53-54], *Sher-E-Punjab Pty Ltd ('Sher-E-Punjab') v Australian Skills Quality Authority* [2018] AATA 46 (15 January 2018) [104-106].
[32] *Business Institute of Australia Pty Ltd ('Business Institute') v Australian Skills Quality Authority* [2019] AATA 669 (16 April 2019) 11 [30], *'Technical Education Australia'* [107], *Metro College of Technology Pty Ltd and Australian Skills Quality Authority* (Unreported) [34], *'Trades College Australia'* [27-28].

LEGAL DECISION-MAKING UNDER THE NATIONAL VOCATIONAL EDUCATION AND TRAINING REGULATOR ACT 2011 (CTH): AN INVESTIGATION INTO ACCESS TO MERITS REVIEW

regulatory decisions during stay proceedings. However, it would appear that Tribunal Members have become so acquainted with ASQA's responsibilities (and arguments) that ASQA lawyers no longer refer to this in as much detail as it once used to as a Statement of Facts, Issues and Contentions; these issues will be addressed later in this paper.

In the context of ASQA's regulatory ambition, s 2A of the NVR Act provides a number of outcomes, which are measured annually in ASQA's annual performance review[33]. The very crux of vocational education and training though, producing job ready graduates for, and endorsed by industry, could be seen as a measure or outcome of the success of ASQA's regulatory performance. It would not be uncommon for a student enrolled in a vocational education and training course to

---

[33] ASQA's reporting requirements are detailed in s215 of the *National Vocational Education and Training Regulator Act 2011* (Cth).

LEGAL DECISION-MAKING UNDER THE NATIONAL VOCATIONAL EDUCATION AND TRAINING REGULATOR ACT 2011 (CTH): AN INVESTIGATION INTO ACCESS TO MERITS REVIEW

have as a measurable outcome that they are *'job ready after training that has been endorsed by industry'*. This is aligned with what Braithwaite describes as *'desirable student outcomes'*.[34]

This student outcome though is a different measure and regulatory ambit to what is provided for in the Objects of the NVR Act at s 2A and yet, under the current student-centred audit model, this should be a key focus. This outcome is something that is completely disregarded by ASQA in its legal decision-making.

There are many examples of cases that have come before the Tribunal[35] where graduates have been

---

[34] Valerie Braithwaite, (n 9) [9].

[35] As well as others who were prevented from accessing merits review due to and including some of the reasons outlined in this paper; For example, *Success Fast-Track Pty Ltd v Australian Skills Quality Authority* [2012] AATA 531 (10 August 2012), *Australian Institute of Trades Pty Ltd as trustee for the Institute of Hotel Management Australia v Australian Skills Quality Authority* [2017] AATA 2912 (1 August 2017) and *Pacific Flight Services Pty Ltd v Australian Skills Quality Authority* [2019] AATA 745 (23

LEGAL DECISION-MAKING UNDER THE NATIONAL VOCATIONAL EDUCATION AND TRAINING REGULATOR ACT 2011 (CTH): AN INVESTIGATION INTO ACCESS TO MERITS REVIEW

endorsed by industry as being suitable graduates and employer satisfaction is high or, the provider meets additional licencing and/or accreditation requirements, yet this evidence is completely disregarded by ASQA and considered irrelevant. The relevance of meeting additional licencing requirements and not ASQA's was an issue discussed by Senior Member Puplick in *Pacific Flight Services v Australian Skills Quality Authority*[36] where the Member states that 'the Tribunal does not accept that there are such inconsistencies between ASQA and CASA regulations and requirements that it is legitimate to give priority to one over the other'.[37]

However, if CASA as the aviation regulator has no concern over the training and assessment practices of the provider and yet ASQA does, the inconsistencies that Senior Member Puplick refers to must exist.

April 2019).
[36] *Pacific Flight Services v Australian Skills Quality Authority* [2019] AATA 745 (23 April 2019).
[37] Ibid at [4].

LEGAL DECISION-MAKING UNDER THE NATIONAL VOCATIONAL EDUCATION AND TRAINING REGULATOR ACT 2011 (CTH): AN INVESTIGATION INTO ACCESS TO MERITS REVIEW

In summary, while COAG's intention for there to be a uniform and consistent framework across all jurisdictions, it is clear that this has still not been achieved and there remains significant tension in the ability of the sector to achieve it. The ambition of Australia's regulatory framework in the VET/IE sector and ASQA's role and operation is to ensure that there is a consistent quality framework that guides its operation; providing monitoring mechanisms and accountability to the public and government. How it goes about achieving this however, and how that performance is measured is something that requires further investigation and discussion.

LEGAL DECISION-MAKING UNDER THE NATIONAL VOCATIONAL EDUCATION AND TRAINING REGULATOR ACT 2011 (CTH): AN INVESTIGATION INTO ACCESS TO MERITS REVIEW

Legal Decision-Making Under the National Vocational Education and Training Regulator Act 2011

The context of this research is focussed primarily on legal decision-making by ASQA and the AAT in relation to merits review. There have been very few formal studies published[38] in relation to ASQA since it was established on 1 July 2011 and it would appear no formal, published research exists in relation to legal decision-making processes and merits review under the NVR Act. The legislative framework that underpins the sector is almost as complex as the regulatory environment itself. At its most basic level, the legislative framework includes (but is not restricted to):

- *National Vocational Education and Training Regulator Act 2011* (Cth);

---

[38] Pricewaterhouse Coopers, (n 19), Valerie Braithwaite, (n 9), The Hon. Steven Joyce, *Strengthening Skills: Expert Review of Australia's Vocational Education and Training System*, (April 2019).

LEGAL DECISION-MAKING UNDER THE NATIONAL VOCATIONAL EDUCATION AND TRAINING REGULATOR ACT 2011 (CTH): AN INVESTIGATION INTO ACCESS TO MERITS REVIEW

- *Standards for Registered Training Organisations (RTOs) 2015* (Cth) ("Standards for RTOs");

- *Fit and Proper Person Requirements 2011* (Cth);

- *Financial Viability Risk Assessment Requirements 2011* (Cth);

- *Data Provision Requirements 2012* (Cth);

- Australian Qualifications Framework, 2nd Edition;[39]

- *Education Services for Overseas Students Act 2000* (Cth) ("ESOS Act");

- *Standards for VET Accredited Courses 2012* (Cth);

- *Standards for VET Regulators 2015* (Cth) ("Standards for VET Regulators");

- *ELICOS Standards 2018* (Cth);[40]

- *Foundation Program Standards.*[41]

---

[39] On its own, the AQF is not a legislative instrument, however, as part of the VET Quality Framework that is referred to in the NVR Act 2011, it now has legal effect for those providers regulated under the VET Quality Framework.

[40] A legislative instrument made under the ESOS Act.

[41] A legislative instrument is made under the ESOS Act.

LEGAL DECISION-MAKING UNDER THE NATIONAL VOCATIONAL EDUCATION AND TRAINING REGULATOR ACT 2011 (CTH): AN INVESTIGATION INTO ACCESS TO MERITS REVIEW

This research also considers the following legislation as it applies to the legal decision-making process under the NVR Act:

- *Administrative Appeals Tribunal Act 1975* (Cth) ("AAT Act");

- *Administrative Decisions (Judicial Review) Act 1977* (Cth);

- *Legal Services Directions 2017* (Cth).[42]

Of the few published reports,[43] a review into the efficacy of the regulator's role was considered with the findings being highly relevant to this research and often referred to nationally in the education and training sector and the media.

The report by PwC,[44] although slightly dated, provided a basis for substantial new funding from the

---

[42] Specifically, app B.
[43] Pricewaterhouse Coopers, (n 19), Valerie Braithwaite, (n 9), The Hon. Steven Joyce, (n 38).

LEGAL DECISION-MAKING UNDER THE
NATIONAL VOCATIONAL EDUCATION AND
TRAINING REGULATOR ACT 2011 (CTH): AN
INVESTIGATION INTO ACCESS TO MERITS
REVIEW

Commonwealth and ASQA's current position as a full cost recovery regulator.[45] The Braithwaite report[46] considers the sector on a much broader scale while also integrating findings on the regulator's ability to improve its effectiveness through enhanced education, training and customer service.

The focus on these issues by Braithwaite was, in some ways, synonymous with some of the things identified through this paper that ASQA must improve to achieve the objectives of the NVR Act.[47]

The more recent Joyce report,[48] was controversial in the sector due to its effective 'reproduction' of the same or

---

[44] Pricewaterhouse Coopers, (n 19).

[45] Australian Skills Quality Authority, *'National Vocational Education and Training Regulator Fees and Charges for Registration of Training Organisations, Accreditation of Courses and Associated Services 2017-18 Consultation DRAFT'* (online at 24 June 2019)
<https://www.asqa.gov.au/file/8046/download?token=qSqaouUX>.

[46] Valerie Braithwaite, (n 9).

[47] NVR Act, (n 16) s 2A.

[48] The Hon. Steven Joyce, (n 38).

LEGAL DECISION-MAKING UNDER THE NATIONAL VOCATIONAL EDUCATION AND TRAINING REGULATOR ACT 2011 (CTH): AN INVESTIGATION INTO ACCESS TO MERITS REVIEW

similar recommendations as the Braithwaite report which came at a significant cost to Australian tax-payers. For many of those involved in the vocational education and training sector were looking forward to finally having an opportunity for VET[49] to be placed under the spotlight and to have some of the issues raised in the Braithwaite review further investigated; it seems though to be another lost opportunity.

The Joyce Review[50] provides an account of how, with media pressure and increased funding, political intervention tends to have a less than ideal impact on meaningful change but rather just rehashes the past; a constant concern of the VET/IE sector generally.[51]

---

[49] As opposed to the NVR Act in the Braithwaite review.

[50] The Hon. Steven Joyce, (n 38).

[51] Historical analysis of the quality standards in the VET sector, in particular, demonstrates that quality standards review is cyclic; there will be a repeat of implementation of standards under the premise of change but it really is just rehashing old policies and standards and dressing them up as something new.

LEGAL DECISION-MAKING UNDER THE NATIONAL VOCATIONAL EDUCATION AND TRAINING REGULATOR ACT 2011 (CTH): AN INVESTIGATION INTO ACCESS TO MERITS REVIEW

It is critical to review the legal decision-making model within ASQA as a way of determining the effectiveness of those legal decisions because so much of that process is the foundation upon which the merits review process at the AAT is based.[52]

Once a decision to sanction has been made under the NVR Act,[53] a provider can seek merits review[54] through the AAT (which will be explored later in this paper). The Tribunal is then required to consider a legal decision that has already been made, whether or not that decision was made effectively or not. The Tribunal Member's task subsequently becomes more problematic when a provider is requesting that the Tribunal Member use

---

[52] Pricewaterhouse Coopers, (n 19), Valerie Braithwaite, (n 9), The Hon. Steven Joyce, (n 38).
[53] NVR Act s 36
[54] For reviewable decisions under the NVR Act.

LEGAL DECISION-MAKING UNDER THE NATIONAL VOCATIONAL EDUCATION AND TRAINING REGULATOR ACT 2011 (CTH): AN INVESTIGATION INTO ACCESS TO MERITS REVIEW

their discretionary powers[55] to, in effect, place a hold on ASQA's decision, while the review takes place.

This task is complicated because of the process involved in making the original legal decision as well as the qualifications, skills, knowledge and experience of those engaged in the legal decision-making process that is under review. In accordance with s 2A of the AAT Act, the Tribunal's objective in carrying out its functions are that:

> ...the Tribunal must pursue the objective of providing a mechanism of review that:
>
> (a) is accessible; and
>
> (b) is fair, just, economical, informal and quick; and
>
> (c) is proportionate to the importance and complexity of the matter; ad

---

[55] AAT Act s 41(2).

LEGAL DECISION-MAKING UNDER THE NATIONAL VOCATIONAL EDUCATION AND TRAINING REGULATOR ACT 2011 (CTH): AN INVESTIGATION INTO ACCESS TO MERITS REVIEW

(d) promotes public trust and confidence in the decision-making of the Tribunal.

It is argued throughout this paper that while the Tribunal would appear to rely upon, or, have an expectation that, the legal decisions being made by ASQA are based on a solid foundation, in many cases, they are not.

Tribunal Members might be experienced in matters of law, but they are not experts in the vocational education and training sector; they do not understand the basis upon which these decisions are being made, nor do they have an understanding of the impact of ASQA's flawed legal decision-making processes. They cannot understand the impact that this flawed legal decision-making has on ASQA's ability to achieve its objectives under the NVR Act. Tribunal Members are unlikely to also understand how this then compromises the Tribunal's ability to achieve its objectives with the AAT

LEGAL DECISION-MAKING UNDER THE NATIONAL VOCATIONAL EDUCATION AND TRAINING REGULATOR ACT 2011 (CTH): AN INVESTIGATION INTO ACCESS TO MERITS REVIEW

Act because it has rightly expected at all times that the basis upon which ASQA's legal decisions were being made was irreproachable.

A clear example of this is found in *Claredale Academy Pty Ltd v Australian Skills Quality Authority*,[56] where Member Parker affirmed ASQA's decision to renew Claredale's NVR Act and ESOS Act registrations.

The underpinning decision-making in relation to Claredale's compliance with Standard 1 for example is extraordinary.

Had Member Parker and the Tribunal been assisted by an independent expert in relation to this issue (as an example of many), the Tribunal might have arrived a completely different correct and preferable decision;

---

[56] *Claredale Academy Pty Ltd v Australian Skills Quality Authority* [2019] AATA 1869 (12 July 2019).

LEGAL DECISION-MAKING UNDER THE NATIONAL VOCATIONAL EDUCATION AND TRAINING REGULATOR ACT 2011 (CTH): AN INVESTIGATION INTO ACCESS TO MERITS REVIEW

albeit, there were other issues of alleged non-compliance which might have still produced the same outcome overall.

The reported decision in *Claredale Academy Pty Ltd v Australian Skills Quality Authority*[57] states that Claredale had failed to comply with Standards[58] 1.3, 1.6, 2.3 and 8.1. At [35], it is reported that 'ASQA found Claredale to be compliant with clause 1.8 of Standard 1, which related to its assessment systems for all its courses'. For an RTO to be compliant with clause 1.8, it is not possible for it to be not compliant with clause 1.3 or 1.6. For the purposes of clarity and transparency in this assertion, clauses 1.8, 1.6 and 1.3 are produced with emphasis by the writer on critical terms, below.

Clause 1.8 states:

---

[57] At [7(a)]
[58] *Standards for Registered Training Organisations 2015* (Cth).

LEGAL DECISION-MAKING UNDER THE NATIONAL VOCATIONAL EDUCATION AND TRAINING REGULATOR ACT 2011 (CTH): AN INVESTIGATION INTO ACCESS TO MERITS REVIEW

1.8. The RTO implements **an assessment system** that ensures that **assessment** (including recognition of prior learning):

a) **complies with the assessment requirements of the relevant training package** or VET accredited course; and

b) is **conducted in accordance with the Principles of Assessment** contained in Table 1.8-1 **and the Rules of Evidence** contained in Table 1.8-2.

LEGAL DECISION-MAKING UNDER THE
NATIONAL VOCATIONAL EDUCATION AND
TRAINING REGULATOR ACT 2011 (CTH): AN
INVESTIGATION INTO ACCESS TO MERITS
REVIEW

Table 1.8-1: Principles of Assessment

Fairness	**The individual learner's needs are considered** in the assessment process.
	Where appropriate, reasonable adjustments are applied by the RTO **to take into account the individual learner's needs.**
	The RTO informs the learner about the assessment process, and provides the learner with the opportunity to challenge the result of the assessment and be reassessed if necessary.
Flexibility	Assessment is flexible to the individual learner by:
	· **reflecting the learner's needs;**
	· **assessing competencies held by the learner no matter how or where they have been acquired;** and
	· drawing from a range of assessment methods and **using those that are appropriate to the context, the unit of competency** and **associated assessment requirements, and the individual.**

LEGAL DECISION-MAKING UNDER THE
NATIONAL VOCATIONAL EDUCATION AND
TRAINING REGULATOR ACT 2011 (CTH): AN
INVESTIGATION INTO ACCESS TO MERITS
REVIEW

Validity	Any assessment decision of the RTO is justified, based on the evidence of performance of the individual learner. Validity requires: · assessment **against the unit/s of competency** and the **associated assessment requirements** covers the broad range of skills and knowledge that are essential to competent performance; · assessment of knowledge and skills is integrated with their practical application; · assessment to be based on evidence that demonstrates that a learner could demonstrate these skills and knowledge in other similar situations; and · judgement of competence is based on evidence of learner performance that is **aligned to the unit/s of competency** and **associated assessment requirements**.
Reliability	Evidence presented for assessment is consistently interpreted and assessment results are comparable irrespective of the assessor conducting the assessment.

LEGAL DECISION-MAKING UNDER THE
NATIONAL VOCATIONAL EDUCATION AND
TRAINING REGULATOR ACT 2011 (CTH): AN
INVESTIGATION INTO ACCESS TO MERITS
REVIEW

Table 1.8-2: Rules of Evidence

Validity	The **assessor is assured** that the learner has the skills, knowledge and attributes as described in the module or **unit of competency** and **associated assessment requirements.**
Sufficiency	The **assessor is assured** that the **quality, quantity and relevance of the assessment evidence** enables a judgement to be made of a learner's competency.
Authenticity	The **assessor is assured** that the evidence presented for assessment is the learner's own work.
Currency	The **assessor is assured** that the assessment evidence demonstrates current competency. This requires the assessment evidence to be from the present or the very recent past.

LEGAL DECISION-MAKING UNDER THE
NATIONAL VOCATIONAL EDUCATION AND
TRAINING REGULATOR ACT 2011 (CTH): AN
INVESTIGATION INTO ACCESS TO MERITS
REVIEW

Clause 1.6 states:

> 1.6. The RTO implements a range of strategies for **industry engagement** and **systematically uses the outcome of that industry engagement** to ensure the **industry relevance** of:
>
> a)   its training and **assessment strategies, practices and resources**; and
>
> b)   the **current industry skills of its trainers and assessors**.

If assessment has not been developed in accordance with this clause, it is impossible for it to be compliant with clause 1.8. As previously demonstrated, as per the glossary provided in the Standards, an assessment system 'is a coordinated set of documented policies and procedures (including assessment materials and tools) that ensure assessments are consistent and based on the Principles of Assessment contained in Table 1.8-1 and the Rules of Evidence contained in Table 1.8-2'.

LEGAL DECISION-MAKING UNDER THE NATIONAL VOCATIONAL EDUCATION AND TRAINING REGULATOR ACT 2011 (CTH): AN INVESTIGATION INTO ACCESS TO MERITS REVIEW

If ASQA has identified that the assessment system has not been developed by using a range of strategies for industry engagement and systematically used the outcome of that engagement in the development and implementation of its assessment system, then it cannot possibly be compliant at clause 1.8. Likewise, if the industry currency of trainers and assessors is allegedly not compliant at 1.6, it follows that the assessment undertaken in accordance with clause 1.8 cannot possibly be compliant either.

Clause 1.3 of the legislative instrument states:

1.3. The RTO has, for all of its scope of registration, and consistent with its training **and assessment strategies**, sufficient:

    a)   **trainers and assessors to deliver** the training and **assessment**;

    b)   educational and support services to **meet the needs of the learner** cohort/s **undertaking the** training and **assessment**;

LEGAL DECISION-MAKING UNDER THE NATIONAL VOCATIONAL EDUCATION AND TRAINING REGULATOR ACT 2011 (CTH): AN INVESTIGATION INTO ACCESS TO MERITS REVIEW

c) learning resources to enable learners to meet the requirements for each unit of competency, and which are accessible to the learner regardless of location or mode of delivery; and

d) facilities, whether physical or virtual, and equipment to accommodate and support the number of learners undertaking the training and assessment.

In interpreting and analysing the highlighted elements of clause 1.3 above, it is clear that if an RTO is not compliant with this clause, it cannot possibly be compliant with clause 1.8. For example, if the RTO is allegedly not compliant with 1.3(a), it's trainers and assessors cannot deliver assessment that complies with clause 1.8. Likewise, if the trainers and assessors are allegedly not compliant with clause 1.3(b) then it is not possible that the assessment conducted under clause 1.8 is compliant.

LEGAL DECISION-MAKING UNDER THE NATIONAL VOCATIONAL EDUCATION AND TRAINING REGULATOR ACT 2011 (CTH): AN INVESTIGATION INTO ACCESS TO MERITS REVIEW

These are just some examples of the complexity of the legal decisions that are being made and how, unless they were also experts in this specialised area of education and training, Tribunal Members cannot possibly arrive at the correct and preferable decision. Tribunal Members are required to maintain impartiality and seek independent expert advice where required to understand the intricacies and complexities of the area under review. What this paper clearly demonstrates is that historically, Tribunal Members have assumed that the legal and reviewable decisions being made by the Commonwealth Regulator ASQA are more likely to be sound. However, this paper also highlights that ASQA as a regulator actually makes highly questionable legal decisions.

Until the Tribunal and its respective members who review ASQA matters have a better understanding of the

LEGAL DECISION-MAKING UNDER THE NATIONAL VOCATIONAL EDUCATION AND TRAINING REGULATOR ACT 2011 (CTH): AN INVESTIGATION INTO ACCESS TO MERITS REVIEW

process in which these legal decisions are being made, it fails to achieve any of its four objectives because:

(a) A Tribunal Member that does not understand or seek to understand the area that they are being asked to review should seek independent expert reports and opinions as a matter of practice to ensure that its decisions are fair, just, economical, informal and quick. A Tribunal Member does not have the expertise (nor should they have) to understand the complexities of this sector. However, in order to be accessible and to achieve its objectives, it is reasonable to expect that the Tribunal Member would seek independent expert advice for the purposes of assisting them to reach its decisions;

(b) Where a Tribunal Member is making decisions without the independent expert advice referred to in the previous point, it is not carrying out its

LEGAL DECISION-MAKING UNDER THE
NATIONAL VOCATIONAL EDUCATION AND
TRAINING REGULATOR ACT 2011 (CTH): AN
INVESTIGATION INTO ACCESS TO MERITS
REVIEW

functions in accordance with s 2A(c) of the AAT Act to be fair, just, economical, informal and quick. All stakeholders would benefit from such an approach because if it were adopted at the very beginning of the AAT process, it would prevent the unnecessary dragging out of matters beyond durations ordinarily expected for a Tribunal matter.[59] By ensuring matters are not unnecessarily dragged out, the process becomes fairer, more just, more economical, more informal because it means less cases are likely to proceed to a full hearing and consequently, achieve faster resolution;

---

[59] The AAT website provides that where a decision is not provided on the day of the hearing, it will usually send a notice of the decision and the written reasons for the decision within 2 months of the hearing. It is not uncommon in the General Division where ASQA matters are heard for decisions to be reserved. It is also not uncommon for notices of decisions and the written reasons for those decisions to be delayed far beyond 2 months.

LEGAL DECISION-MAKING UNDER THE NATIONAL VOCATIONAL EDUCATION AND TRAINING REGULATOR ACT 2011 (CTH): AN INVESTIGATION INTO ACCESS TO MERITS REVIEW

(c) By not adopting independent expert assistance to understand the complexity of the matters under review, the Tribunal is unwittingly reducing the level of importance being attributed to these matters and dismissing the level of complexity involved. For many training providers accessing merits review at the AAT, the importance and complexity of their matters is far greater than the current process allows consideration for. ASQA, under the umbrella of exercising its duties under the NVR Act, often complicates the process for applicants and the Tribunal. ASQA often does not comply with the General Direction of the Tribunal yet pounces of the legal representatives of the applicant if their legal representative is slightly delayed for any reason for example, and has been known to engage in behaviour that is

52

LEGAL DECISION-MAKING UNDER THE
NATIONAL VOCATIONAL EDUCATION AND
TRAINING REGULATOR ACT 2011 (CTH): AN
INVESTIGATION INTO ACCESS TO MERITS
REVIEW

inconsistent with the General Direction of the Tribunal and the Model Litigant Guideline.;[60]

(d) By not adopting the suggestions outlined, the public trust and confidence in the decision-making of the Tribunal is compromised, this aligns with the findings made by the Honourable Ian Callinan AC in his recent review of the AAT.[61]

---

[60] As found in the *Legal Services Directions 2017* (Cth)
[61] Hon Ian Callinan AC, *Review: Section 4 of the Tribunals Amalgamation Act 2015 (Cth) Report*, (July 2019).

LEGAL DECISION-MAKING UNDER THE
NATIONAL VOCATIONAL EDUCATION AND
TRAINING REGULATOR ACT 2011 (CTH): AN
INVESTIGATION INTO ACCESS TO MERITS
REVIEW

Conduct of audits

The NVR Act provides for the Standards for VET Regulators[62] which have the following purpose:

To ensure:

- the integrity of nationally recognised training by regulating RTOs and VET accredited courses using a risk-based approach that is consistent, effective, proportional, responsive and transparent;

- consistency in the VET Regulator's implementation and interpretation of the RTO Standards and Standards for VET Accredited Courses; and

- the accountability and transparency of the VET Regulator in undertaking its regulatory functions.

---

[62] *Standards for VET Regulators 2015* made under ss 189(1) of the *National Vocational Education and Training Regulator Act 2011* (Cth).

LEGAL DECISION-MAKING UNDER THE NATIONAL VOCATIONAL EDUCATION AND TRAINING REGULATOR ACT 2011 (CTH): AN INVESTIGATION INTO ACCESS TO MERITS REVIEW

The term *'auditor'* is defined under these Standards[63] with Standard 1 providing a reference to the national competency standard for auditors[64] engaged by the national regulator for performing some of its functions as a regulator, including that the 'VET Regulator makes decisions consistent with the principles of natural justice and procedural fairness'.[65]

---

[63] Ibid, see the Glossary at Annexure A 'auditor'.
[64] *Standards for VET Regulators*, Standard 1.9(c), sch 1.
[65] Ibid, Standard 1.10.

LEGAL DECISION-MAKING UNDER THE NATIONAL VOCATIONAL EDUCATION AND TRAINING REGULATOR ACT 2011 (CTH): AN INVESTIGATION INTO ACCESS TO MERITS REVIEW

The Audit Process

ASQA is empowered under various sections[66] of the NVR Act to conduct audits in order to perform some of its functions as the National VET Regulator.[67] ASQA engages various staff and consultants to undertake these regulatory functions, including audits in accordance with ss 182-184 of the Act. While ASQA does use its own staff where possible to conduct its regulatory functions, in the 2017/2018 Annual Report, ASQA spent $968,000 on its panel auditors and a further $687,000 on *'Consultants'*.

The same report states that 'The consultancy contracts were for a range of services including internal and external audit and financial management'.[68]

---

[66] The NVR Act provides for audits under s 17(3) and s 35, in the performance of its duties under s 33(a)(c). Division 2 of the Act provides for investigations and searches of premises.
[67] NVR Act s 157.
[68] Australian Skills Quality Authority, *ASQA Annual Report 2017-2018*, 106.

LEGAL DECISION-MAKING UNDER THE NATIONAL VOCATIONAL EDUCATION AND TRAINING REGULATOR ACT 2011 (CTH): AN INVESTIGATION INTO ACCESS TO MERITS REVIEW

These costs to the Australian taxpayer were again considered later in this report in the context of *'the public interest'*.

Regulatory audits can be triggered by any range of events in addition to those identified for the purposes or registration and change of scope of registration. They can be triggered for factors including, but not limited to issues such as:

- a provider seeking to add a new delivery location;
- a provider seeking to increase their student capacity;
- ASQA's receipt of complaints;
- general compliance monitoring;
- national strategic reviews; or, as previously referred to,
- an investigation.

What follows is a general overview of the audit process under ASQA.

LEGAL DECISION-MAKING UNDER THE NATIONAL VOCATIONAL EDUCATION AND TRAINING REGULATOR ACT 2011 (CTH): AN INVESTIGATION INTO ACCESS TO MERITS REVIEW

While audits are a standard requirement for many institutions, both public and private to maintain standards, in the current ASQA regulatory environment, audits are generally triggered as opposed to being a part of standard operating procedure.

The audit process usually begins with a desktop review of the evidence (in some cases, the audit may actually end there because a legal decision has already been made to reject or cancel registration for example).[69] The audit will usually be conducted by an ASQA panel auditor or an ASQA Regulatory Officer. A finding will generally be made that the level of non-compliance is minor, serious or critical although, in recent months, a new finding is being made of *'concerning compliance'*.

---

[69] Providers may at this point receive one of a number of *'Notices'* from ASQA including, for example, a *'Notice of intention to impose a sanction'* or a *'Notice of intention to cancel registration'*; Since 1 July 2018, applicants for initial registration as an RTO are issued with a 'Notice' rejecting their application for any non-compliance.

LEGAL DECISION-MAKING UNDER THE NATIONAL VOCATIONAL EDUCATION AND TRAINING REGULATOR ACT 2011 (CTH): AN INVESTIGATION INTO ACCESS TO MERITS REVIEW

Historically, ASQA would provide RTOs who had been deemed not compliant with 20 working days to rectify any non-compliance identified at audit. ASQA has in recent times suggested that this was a discretionary power that it *'volunteered'* and was not obliged by law to provide. On 1 July 2018, ASQA removed this option for applications for initial registration. Where a legal decision has not been made after completion of the desktop audit, a site visit will be conducted; these are usually performed by the same auditor who undertook the desktop audit.

The auditor will then usually make a recommendation which is communicated to the Manager of Regulatory Operations in the relevant jurisdiction who will then approve the audit report for release. The correspondence can either be in the form of a provision of 20 working days to rectify any non-compliance or, the issue of a Notice.[70] In either case, the provider will

LEGAL DECISION-MAKING UNDER THE NATIONAL VOCATIONAL EDUCATION AND TRAINING REGULATOR ACT 2011 (CTH): AN INVESTIGATION INTO ACCESS TO MERITS REVIEW

typically have 20 working days in which to respond to the audit report (and if relevant, the Notice) and they may provide new evidence to be considered at this point. The evidence may or may not be reviewed by the same auditor or regulatory officer.

Upon consideration of the response, ASQA will make a new decision that either the provider is compliant, and no further action is taken, alternatively, they may issue a Notice[71] if one wasn't previously or confirm the previous Notice. If the Notice is affirmed, the provider then has access to external review[72] provisions under the NVR Act[73] if it is a reviewable decision[74] under that Act. ASQA summarises this process as follows:

---

[70] Ibid.

[71] Ibid.

[72] Providers also have access to internal review mechanisms however they do not form part of this research.

[73] NVR Act s 203.

[74] Ibid s 199.

LEGAL DECISION-MAKING UNDER THE NATIONAL VOCATIONAL EDUCATION AND TRAINING REGULATOR ACT 2011 (CTH): AN INVESTIGATION INTO ACCESS TO MERITS REVIEW

Responsibility for regulatory decisions by ASQA resides with its Commissioners, with some decisions being made jointly by all three Commissioners, and others by a single Commissioner or senior staff holding a delegation...The streaming of decisions will be based upon an analysis of a range of factors, including:

- how serious the impact of the decision may be on the VET industry and its reputation, and

- whether ASQA has identified serious concerns about the provider in question.

Decisions which have the most severe impact on a training provider such as cancellation or non-renewal of registration will generally be made jointly by all three Commissioners, while decisions with a lesser impact will usually be

LEGAL DECISION-MAKING UNDER THE NATIONAL VOCATIONAL EDUCATION AND TRAINING REGULATOR ACT 2011 (CTH): AN INVESTIGATION INTO ACCESS TO MERITS REVIEW

made by a single Commissioner or a senior staff member holding delegated authority.

If a decision is made jointly by ASQA's Commissioners, a review of that decision can only be made by an external authority (such as the Administrative Appeals Tribunal). In these cases, the provider cannot apply for an internal ASQA reconsideration of the decision…

Amendments to the *Education Services for Overseas Students Act 2000* (Cth) (ESOS Act), which took effect on 1 July 2016, enable ASQA to delegate certain CRICOS decisions, which previously had to be made jointly by all three Commissioners.[75]

The ASQA website clearly states that the decision will be made jointly by all three Commissioners, however,

---

[75] Australian Skills Authority, '*Changes to ASQA's Decision-Making Processes*', (Web Page) <https://www.asqa.gov.au/news-publications/media/asqa-announces-further-changes-protect-sectorhttps://www.asqa.gov.au/news-publications/media/asqa-announces-further-changes-protect-sector>.

LEGAL DECISION-MAKING UNDER THE NATIONAL VOCATIONAL EDUCATION AND TRAINING REGULATOR ACT 2011 (CTH): AN INVESTIGATION INTO ACCESS TO MERITS REVIEW

the standard correspondence that a provider will receive from ASQA in the *'most severe of circumstances'* reads somewhat differently.

The generic template letter[76] that will usually be issued to a provider in the *'most severe of circumstances'* provides 'In accordance with section 37(2) of the NVR Act, ASQA hereby gives you notice that the *Chief Commissioner for the Commissioners (as opposed to three Commissioners as stated on the ASQA website)* has made a decision to cancel your registration under section 39 with effect from…'.[77]

However, some RTOs receive a very different letter[78] regarding the decision to cancel their registration which

---

[76] The generic template letter referred to is the standard correspondence received by providers. The example used however is 'Letter from Benn Gramola to Name Withheld, 29 May 2019 [3]'.

[77] Australian Skills Quality Authority, *'Notice of Decision to Cancel NVR Act Registration'* template (no version number, date).

[78] Letter from Benn Gramola to Name Withheld, 29 March 2019 [3], professional correspondence held on client's file - RTO Doctor, at 23 January 2019 [3], professional correspondence held on client's file - RTO Doctor, at 15 January 2019 [2], at 22 November 2018 [2], at 11

LEGAL DECISION-MAKING UNDER THE NATIONAL VOCATIONAL EDUCATION AND TRAINING REGULATOR ACT 2011 (CTH): AN INVESTIGATION INTO ACCESS TO MERITS REVIEW

is completely at odds with the explanation provided by ASQA and states 'In accordance with section 37(2) of the NVR Act, ASQA hereby gives you notice that *it* (*as opposed to the three Commissioners or the Chief Commissioner on behalf of the three Commissioners as per the previous point*) has made a decision to cancel your registration under section 39 with effect from 29 April 2019'. All cases referred to were eligible for external review and all correspondence was issued by the same staff member.

The Braithwaite report[79] identified that 'there is a real need for transparency around ASQA audits to inform the sector on where systemic weaknesses lie'. The issues presented in this paper are only the tip of the iceberg; there are sadly many more that still require investigation.

April 2018 [3], at 30 August 2017 [3], at 11 August 2017 [2].
[79] Valerie Braithwaite, (n 9) 8 [3].

LEGAL DECISION-MAKING UNDER THE NATIONAL VOCATIONAL EDUCATION AND TRAINING REGULATOR ACT 2011 (CTH): AN INVESTIGATION INTO ACCESS TO MERITS REVIEW

The writer submits that from an ethical standpoint at least, there is an obligation on the Commonwealth, in particular, the Attorney-General and the relevant Ministers, to investigate these matters further. Some of the additional critical concerns that have not been discussed in this paper that require further investigation include for example, but are not limited to:

- Auditors can be deemed by the Regulator to be beyond reproach in their decision-making and findings related to the level of compliance of providers that leads to Notices and sanctions under the Act when contracted by ASQA. Yet, when presenting evidence on behalf of RTO clients in their capacity of private Consultants, ASQA dismisses the validity and reliability of their evidence and the Tribunal subsequently considers their opinions differently.

LEGAL DECISION-MAKING UNDER THE NATIONAL VOCATIONAL EDUCATION AND TRAINING REGULATOR ACT 2011 (CTH): AN INVESTIGATION INTO ACCESS TO MERITS REVIEW

- Is there a conflict of interest where ASQA auditors are also acting as rectification Consultants for RTOs who are deemed allegedly not compliant by ASQA?

- The Honourable Ian Callinan in his recent review of the AAT[80] stated that the acting head of ASQA referred to "'ghost colleges", little more than addresses operated by people who provided no real training or tuition'. This statement was denied by ASQA[81] publicly however, this is an argument that ASQA lawyers often use and refer to in Tribunal proceedings.[82] This suggests that

---

[80] Hon Ian Callinan AC, *Review: Section 4 of the Tribunals Amalgamation Act 2015 (Cth) Report*, (July 2019) [at 6.96].

[81] Tim Dodd, 'Regulator Denies Ghost College Claims', *The Australian* (online, 25 July 2019) 5 < https://www.theaustralian.com.au/higher-education/regulator-denies-ghost-college-claims/news-story/38b7c6e9ed9d426743fe37e6374d0499>

[82] *Sher-E-Punjab Pty Ltd v Australian Skills Quality Authority* (n 31), *Australian Institute of Technical Training Pty Ltd v Minister for Education and Training* (n 31) and *Business Institute of Australia Pty Ltd v Australian Skills Quality Authority* (n 32).

LEGAL DECISION-MAKING UNDER THE NATIONAL VOCATIONAL EDUCATION AND TRAINING REGULATOR ACT 2011 (CTH): AN INVESTIGATION INTO ACCESS TO MERITS REVIEW

the view is held by more than those litigating on behalf of the Commonwealth but is representative of a culture of belief within the regulatory body itself.

- In the context of the issues highlighted in this paper, and those yet to be investigated but recommended for further review, what is the public interest that both ASQA and the AAT are desperately trying to protect in accordance with their legislated objectives?

One of the key findings of this research is that there needs to be more transparency about the audit process and the legal decisions being made at all points in the legal decision-making process. This would ensure that the foundation upon which external review is being sought is not only sound but legally valid and reliable.

LEGAL DECISION-MAKING UNDER THE NATIONAL VOCATIONAL EDUCATION AND TRAINING REGULATOR ACT 2011 (CTH): AN INVESTIGATION INTO ACCESS TO MERITS REVIEW

LEGAL DECISION-MAKING UNDER THE NATIONAL VOCATIONAL EDUCATION AND TRAINING REGULATOR ACT 2011 (CTH): AN INVESTIGATION INTO ACCESS TO MERITS REVIEW

What is a legal decision?

The definition of a legal decision is critical because the vast majority of Standards that are being audited under s 35 of the NVR Act are in fact statutes. The legislative framework that underpins the sector described earlier includes legislative instruments made under the NVR Act[83] such as the Standards for RTOs.

Despite these Standards[84] being legislative instruments and therefore for the purposes of the Tribunal, primary materials, it would appear that they are systematically reported by the Tribunal as secondary materials, perhaps

---

[83] NVR Act s 231A.

[84] The two main legislative instruments that are erroneously reported as secondary sources are the Standards for RTOs (n 58), National Code (n 30); Examples include *'Trades College Australia Pty Ltd'* (n 31), *'Technical Education Australia Pty Ltd'* (n 31), *'Institute of Training Pty Ltd'* (n 31), *'VETiS Consulting Services Pty Ltd'* (n 31), *'Business Institute of Australia Pty Ltd'* (n 32), *Australian Trade Training and Assessment Pty Ltd (ATTA) v Australian Skills Quality Authority* [2019] AATA 231 (25 January 2019).

LEGAL DECISION-MAKING UNDER THE NATIONAL VOCATIONAL EDUCATION AND TRAINING REGULATOR ACT 2011 (CTH): AN INVESTIGATION INTO ACCESS TO MERITS REVIEW

influencing the emphasis that the Tribunal places on decisions made under them.

Secondary sources are usually reference materials such as 'textbooks, legal encyclopaedias and periodical articles...secondary sources are contrasted with the primary sources of law (cases and legislation)'.[85] By not placing sufficient emphasis on whether the Standards are primary or secondary materials in its legal decision-making, the Tribunal is also erring in its legal decision-making process.

Primary legal materials are those most relied upon in making legal decisions because they contain written records of the law such as legislative instruments and case law.

---

[85] *LexisNexis Concise Australian Legal Dictionary* (5th ed, 2015) 'secondary sources' (def 1,2).

LEGAL DECISION-MAKING UNDER THE NATIONAL VOCATIONAL EDUCATION AND TRAINING REGULATOR ACT 2011 (CTH): AN INVESTIGATION INTO ACCESS TO MERITS REVIEW

Secondary legal materials however provide information, discussion, explanation and analysis about the law.

The Standards for RTOs 2015 for example, as a legislative instrument made under the NVR Act, and the National Code 2018 as a legislative instrument made under the ESOS Act, are primary legal materials. Not only do they appear to be relegated to 'secondary legal materials' by some Tribunal Members, but they are also incorrectly reported as such potentially influencing the weight placed upon their importance in relation to legal decision-making under the Act.[86]

Withnall Howe and Evans[87] state 'a decision is a conclusion that is required to be made under a statute'.

---

[86] Examples include 'Trades College Australia Pty Ltd' (n 31), 'Technical Education Australia Pty Ltd' (n 31), 'Institute of Training Pty Ltd' (n 31), 'VETiS Consulting Services Pty Ltd' (n 31), 'Business Institute of Australia Pty Ltd' (n 32), Australian Trade Training and Assessment Pty Ltd (ATTA) v Australian Skills Quality Authority (n 84), Claredale Academy Pty Ltd v Australian Skills Quality Authority [2019] AATA 1869 (12 July 2019).

LEGAL DECISION-MAKING UNDER THE NATIONAL VOCATIONAL EDUCATION AND TRAINING REGULATOR ACT 2011 (CTH): AN INVESTIGATION INTO ACCESS TO MERITS REVIEW

Importantly, they also state 'It often has an element of finality because when it is made it can be implemented and may affect the rights and interests of the parties'. The AAT Act[88] provides a definition of 'decision' on the basis that the Tribunal 'reviews' a 'decision'.

That definition, for the purposes of this research, includes 'making, suspending, revoking or refusing to make an order or determination',[89] 'issuing, suspending, revoking or refusing to issue a licence, authority or other instrument'[90] or 'imposing a condition or restriction'.[91] It also includes circumstances where decisions are not made.[92] That definition is crucial for this research because if an administrative action (such as those

---

[87] Sarah Withnall Howe and Michelle Evans, *Administrative Law*, (LexisNexis Butterworths, 2nd ed, 2015) 38 [3.7].
[88] AAT Act s 3(3).
[89] Ibid s 3(3)(a).
[90] Ibid s 3(3)(c).
[91] Ibid s 3(3)(d).
[92] Ibid s 3(3)(g).

LEGAL DECISION-MAKING UNDER THE NATIONAL VOCATIONAL EDUCATION AND TRAINING REGULATOR ACT 2011 (CTH): AN INVESTIGATION INTO ACCESS TO MERITS REVIEW

referred to) does not constitute a 'decision' for the purposes of the *Administrative Decisions (Judicial Review) Act 1997* (Cth), it cannot be reviewed. It was also held that a decision is more than the steps along the way to making the final decision. Steps along the way are not to be regarded as constituting decisions yet, the basis upon which many of these legal decisions by ASQA are being made is precisely on the decisions made by the auditor during the audit process. Case law also provides numerous considerations of what a legal decision is and is not; *Australian Broadcasting Tribunal v Bond*,[93] and in the educational space, *Shvetsova v University of New England*,[94] *R v University of Cambridge, Griffith University v Tang*,[95] *Walsh v University of Technology, Sydney*.[96]

---

[93] *Australian Broadcasting Tribunal v Bond* [1990] HCA 33
[94] *Shvetsova V University of New England* [2014] NSWSC 918
[95] *Griffith University v Tang* (2005) 221 CLR 99
[96] *Walsh v University of Technology, Sydney* [2007] FCA 880

LEGAL DECISION-MAKING UNDER THE NATIONAL VOCATIONAL EDUCATION AND TRAINING REGULATOR ACT 2011 (CTH): AN INVESTIGATION INTO ACCESS TO MERITS REVIEW

According to ASQA's website,[97] the VET sector in Australia 'enables students to gain qualifications for all types of employment, and specific skills to help them in the workplace'. This important function is undertaken through the implementation of training packages that are developed to meet the training needs of industry, or a group of industries. Training packages do not suggest how a learner should be trained, rather, they specify the skills and knowledge required to perform effectively in the workplace'.[98] This training is then provided to students by RTOs, both public (usually TAFE) and private.

It is this training and assessment, compliance with the relevant training package and legislation, including its associated legislative instruments[99] that is then audited by those auditors referred to previously.

---

[97] Australian Skills Authority, '*About Australia's VET Sector*', (Web Page) <https://www.asqa.gov.au/about/australias-vet-sector>.
[98] Ibid, Valerie Braithwaite (n 9).
[99] For example, the Standards for RTOs (n 58).

LEGAL DECISION-MAKING UNDER THE NATIONAL VOCATIONAL EDUCATION AND TRAINING REGULATOR ACT 2011 (CTH): AN INVESTIGATION INTO ACCESS TO MERITS REVIEW

A 2018 advertisement[100] for a 'Lead Auditor' for ASQA identified that it is not only **not** mandatory to meet the national competency standard in order to apply for a role as Lead Auditor, but it is not even highly desirable or preferable. The advertisement clearly states that if it is not held upon commencement, the successful incumbent will be expected to obtain it (although no timeframe for completion is provided).

Of critical importance is that auditors performing the functions of the VET Regulator under the NVR Act are therefore required to interpret legislation without being required to hold the requisite knowledge, skills or experience under the Standards for VET Regulators. Additionally, and perhaps just as importantly, auditors

---

[100] Australian Skills Quality Authority, 'APS6 - Lead Auditor', Federal Government Career (Archived Advertisement, 04 May 2018) <federal.governmentcareer.com.au/jobs/8282-australian-skills-quality-authority-asqa/60615>.

LEGAL DECISION-MAKING UNDER THE NATIONAL VOCATIONAL EDUCATION AND TRAINING REGULATOR ACT 2011 (CTH): AN INVESTIGATION INTO ACCESS TO MERITS REVIEW

are not even required to have an area of industry expertise to which their auditing might be attached.

In considering the national competency standard of the VET Regulator under the *Standards for VET Regulators 2015*, it is beneficial to compare it to the national competency standard required of trainers and assessors under the Standards for RTOs. There are certain basic mandatory elements under the Standards for RTOs for trainers and assessors that the VET Regulator does not have, yet arguably should.

These mandatory requirements include for example the need to demonstrate vocational competencies at least to the level being delivered and assessed,[101] current industry skills directly relevant to the training and assessment being provided[102] and current knowledge and skills in

---

[101] Standards for RTOs (n 58), Clause 1.13(a).
[102] Ibid clause 1.13(b).

vocational training and learning that informs their training and assessment.[103]

There is an additional provision for areas that require technical expertise stating, 'Industry experts may also be involved in the assessment judgement, working alongside the trainer and/or assessor to conduct the assessment'.[104]

On the basis that the VET Regulator is auditing providers in relation to their compliance with industry training packages, compliance with the NVR Act and its associated legislative instruments, it is argued that it would not, therefore, be unreasonable to expect that the VET Regulator also meets, at a minimum these same standards.

---

[103] Ibid clause 1.13(c).
[104] Ibid, Clause 1.13.

LEGAL DECISION-MAKING UNDER THE NATIONAL VOCATIONAL EDUCATION AND TRAINING REGULATOR ACT 2011 (CTH): AN INVESTIGATION INTO ACCESS TO MERITS REVIEW

In other words, the VET Regulator, in the conduct of its audits, demonstrates as a national competency standard vocational competencies at least to the level being *audited*, current industry skills directly relevant to the training and assessment being *audited* and current knowledge and skills in vocational training and learning that informs their *auditing*.

This issue was also raised by the applicant in *Pacific Flight Services*. However, the Tribunal Member acknowledged that this was potentially the case although ASQA 'was at pains to point out that the assessor who undertook the Audit was equally as qualified and the Tribunal rejects any suggestion (implicit or otherwise) on the part of the Applicant, via this report, to call into question the professional competency of the ASQA assessor(s) involved'.[105]

---

[105] *Pacific Flight Services Pty Ltd v Australian Skills Quality Authority* (n 35) [at 48].

LEGAL DECISION-MAKING UNDER THE NATIONAL VOCATIONAL EDUCATION AND TRAINING REGULATOR ACT 2011 (CTH): AN INVESTIGATION INTO ACCESS TO MERITS REVIEW

While this paper has no evidence to support or deny the suggestion by the applicant in that matter, however one must question what evidence, if any, was produced by ASQA to contradict the allegation.

Perhaps more importantly, it is open to question on what basis the Tribunal found in one part of paragraph 48 that *'This may very well be the case in terms of the named individual'*[106] yet in the same paragraph, the Tribunal states explicitly that it *'rejects any suggestion* (implicit or otherwise)...*to call into question the professional competency of the ASQA assessor(s) involved*[107]; it just does not make sense.

---

[106] Emphasis added by the writer.
[107] Emphasis added by the writer.

LEGAL DECISION-MAKING UNDER THE NATIONAL VOCATIONAL EDUCATION AND TRAINING REGULATOR ACT 2011 (CTH): AN INVESTIGATION INTO ACCESS TO MERITS REVIEW

There is already an additional provision[108] for the VET Regulator to use technical experts in areas that require specialist knowledge however it would appear that this provision is rarely used. While trainers and assessors are required to hold a relevant training and assessment qualification (or equivalent), the VET Regulator is required to hold certain auditing certification, although, as was demonstrated in the Lead Auditor advertisement, there appears to be flexibility in the application of this standard.

There is no evidence to suggest that any of the auditors engaged by the VET Regulator are legal practitioners with any legal training enabling them to partake in statutory interpretation at a level that would ensure procedural fairness. Procedural fairness is 'a common law principle implied in relation to statutory and prerogative powers to ensure the fairness of the

---

[108] Standards for VET Regulators (n 62) sch 1.

LEGAL DECISION-MAKING UNDER THE NATIONAL VOCATIONAL EDUCATION AND TRAINING REGULATOR ACT 2011 (CTH): AN INVESTIGATION INTO ACCESS TO MERITS REVIEW

decision-making procedure of courts and administrators',[109] yet, on a daily basis, they are performing this task and making recommendations to their managers whose qualifications, knowledge and skills might be in some cases quite similar or even less. PwC in its review of ASQA processes[110] were categoric about the significant training needs that would need to be undertaken for example to incorporate the future (*which now occurs*) implementation of issuing fines and comprehensive training across its audit practices in interview and management techniques.

ASQA line managers also made observations that there were skills deficiencies in complex audit matters and ESOS Act matters, as well as serious skills deficiencies in their investigations team placing significant limitations on their ability to effectively carry out their roles.[111]

---

[109] LexisNexis Butterworths (n 85) 'procedural fairness' (def 1).
[110] Pricewaterhouse Coopers, (n 19) 55.

LEGAL DECISION-MAKING UNDER THE
NATIONAL VOCATIONAL EDUCATION AND
TRAINING REGULATOR ACT 2011 (CTH): AN
INVESTIGATION INTO ACCESS TO MERITS
REVIEW

ASQA's response[112] to these issues at the time was that 'staffing limitations reflect ASQA's budget and commitments under the Transitional Provisions Act to offer positions to state and territory employees'.

The manner in which these underpinning decisions are made is a critical factor in the overall context of how legal decisions under the NVR Act are arrived at, especially in the context of being reviewable decisions by the AAT. It is clear the capacity of the VET Regulator is compromised in its ability to effectuate legal decisions under the NVR Act that are procedurally fair and informed by relevant expertise. What is potentially less clear is whether the external review body understands the lack of expertise and questionable legal decisions being made by and for the VET Regulator.

---

[111] Ibid xi-xii.
[112] Ibid.

LEGAL DECISION-MAKING UNDER THE NATIONAL VOCATIONAL EDUCATION AND TRAINING REGULATOR ACT 2011 (CTH): AN INVESTIGATION INTO ACCESS TO MERITS REVIEW

For the purposes of clarity, a line manager makes a recommendation based on the audit findings of the auditor. When a reviewable decision is being made, it is on the basis of that audit (although it might include consideration of other factors, seldom identified to the provider).

When a Notice of the type referred to earlier is being considered by a line manager, this recommendation is then forwarded to the Commissioner who is required to consider the evidence before them (some of which the provider may not be aware of) before making a decision on the same basis.

These decisions appear to be compromised, procedurally unfair, bordering on procedural ultra vires[113] and not informed by appropriate expertise.

---

[113] Sarah Withnall Howe and Michelle Evans, (n 87) 193-194 [10.3].

LEGAL DECISION-MAKING UNDER THE NATIONAL VOCATIONAL EDUCATION AND TRAINING REGULATOR ACT 2011 (CTH): AN INVESTIGATION INTO ACCESS TO MERITS REVIEW

This situation presents further complications for providers as they attempt to gain access to merits review at the AAT, not least of which are those related to the very reasons why the Tribunal was initially established.[114] The Kerr Committee found in 1971 reported that:

> ... the scope and complexity of government intervention in Australian society had grown greatly since federation and was concerned that review of government decisions through Parliament and the courts had provided an inadequate response. The system was flawed both with regard to substance and accessibility. What was needed, it reported, was an accessible, informal and relatively cheap means for obtaining review of the merits of administrative decisions

---

[114] Administrative Review Committee, Administrative Review Committee Report, Parl Paper No 144 (1971).

LEGAL DECISION-MAKING UNDER THE NATIONAL VOCATIONAL EDUCATION AND TRAINING REGULATOR ACT 2011 (CTH): AN INVESTIGATION INTO ACCESS TO MERITS REVIEW

The AAT today has as an objective as discussed earlier to fill this gap yet what we also saw was its ability to do so in this context at least is compromised.

LEGAL DECISION-MAKING UNDER THE NATIONAL VOCATIONAL EDUCATION AND TRAINING REGULATOR ACT 2011 (CTH): AN INVESTIGATION INTO ACCESS TO MERITS REVIEW

Potential for Review

As referred to several times through this paper, all NVR RTOs have the opportunity for external review[115] for certain decisions[116] made under the NVR Act, namely, those made under s 199. The legislative framework for a stay and a review of a decision by ASQA in the AAT is well documented through case law[117] and previously. The most common applications that are made with the AAT are applications for 'a stay of the decision' and 'a review of the decision'. A decision that is subject to review has full effect and operation unless the Tribunal uses its discretion[118] to make an order to stay the operation and effect of that decision.

---

[115] NVR Act s 203.

[116] Ibid s 199.

[117] For example, *Sydney Training Academy Pty Ltd and Australian Skills Quality Authority* [2018] AATA 3361 (7 September 2018) [18], '*Australian Trade Training and Assessment Pty Ltd (ATTA)*' [14], '*Business Institute of Australia Pty Ltd*' (n 32).

[118] AAT Act s 41(2)

LEGAL DECISION-MAKING UNDER THE NATIONAL VOCATIONAL EDUCATION AND TRAINING REGULATOR ACT 2011 (CTH): AN INVESTIGATION INTO ACCESS TO MERITS REVIEW

What this means in practice for an NVR RTO who has been impacted by a Notice from ASQA is that, at least from a legal perspective, their registration continues until the substantive hearing has been finalised and a new decision made. The external review process at the AAT is a mechanism allowing for a review of the original decision to determine whether the correct or preferable decision was made in the circumstances of that individual case.[119]

The Tribunal is open to receive new evidence, including evidence that was not before the decision-maker at the time the original decision was made.[120]

---

[119] Judith Bannister, Anna Olijnyk and Stephen McDonald, (n 15) 225, Sarah Withnall Howe and Michelle Evans, (n 87) 193-194, Administrative Review Council, *Better Decisions: Review Of The Commonwealth Merits Review Tribunals* (Report to the Minister for Justice No 39, 1995).

[120] There is anecdotal evidence that both ASQA and Tribunal members are frustrated by providers who submit fresh evidence confirming compliance through this process but regardless of their dislike or frustration at this process, it is legally permissible (and expected) outcome of merits review in Australia.

LEGAL DECISION-MAKING UNDER THE NATIONAL VOCATIONAL EDUCATION AND TRAINING REGULATOR ACT 2011 (CTH): AN INVESTIGATION INTO ACCESS TO MERITS REVIEW

The overriding concept that drives this mechanism is that the Tribunal 'stands in the shoes of the original decision-maker' and is able to undertake a fresh review of the decision, a 'hearing de novo'.[121]

The genesis of merits review comes from the Kerr Committee in 1971 who explained that people who have been negatively impacted by Commonwealth or Tribunal decisions will generally feel as though that decision was wrong based on the merits of the case.[122] The Kerr Committee found that it was appropriate to establish a mechanism that was 'accessible (cheap, informal and quick) and responsive to the needs of persons using the system'.[123]

What the Committee also found amongst many other things was that merits review Tribunals in Australia were

---

[121] Sarah Withnall Howe and Michelle Evans, (n 87) 193-194 [2.2], Administrative Review Council, (n 119) viii [1].
[122] Administrative Review Council (n 119).
[123] Ibid 28 [2.11].

LEGAL DECISION-MAKING UNDER THE NATIONAL VOCATIONAL EDUCATION AND TRAINING REGULATOR ACT 2011 (CTH): AN INVESTIGATION INTO ACCESS TO MERITS REVIEW

not operating coherently and in accordance with these objectives. The full finding in relation to this issue is reproduced next as it demonstrates certain points (emphasis added) that will be touched upon next.

...the system of review tribunals can no longer accurately be described as a

coherent system. For example, there are major differences both between and within the

different tribunals in such matters as:

- **the degree of formality of proceedings, including the physical environment and the level of representation;**

- the style of proceedings, including the use of techniques such as decisions 'on the

- papers', mediation, non-adversarial proceedings and **adversarial hearings featuring**

LEGAL DECISION-MAKING UNDER THE NATIONAL VOCATIONAL EDUCATION AND TRAINING REGULATOR ACT 2011 (CTH): AN INVESTIGATION INTO ACCESS TO MERITS REVIEW

- **cross-examination**;
- the mix of skills brought to tribunal panels, including the use of single-member panels;
- the level of information and assistance provided by tribunals and agencies to applicants and to the broader community;
- the method of selecting tribunal members, their terms and conditions of appointment, and the level of professional development and support provided to them;
- the availability and style of internal review within decision-making agencies;
- the methods adopted to ensure that tribunal decisions are considered by agencies in the development of their

LEGAL DECISION-MAKING UNDER THE NATIONAL VOCATIONAL EDUCATION AND TRAINING REGULATOR ACT 2011 (CTH): AN INVESTIGATION INTO ACCESS TO MERITS REVIEW

policy, legislation and decision-making processes; and

- **the cost of the merits review process.**[124]

Those issues highlighted in the extract from the ARC report are emphasised to demonstrate current features of the merits review process in Australia in relation to stay applications for NVR RTOs pursuant to s 203 of the NVR Act and s 41(2) of the AAT Act.

From the 28 reported decisions that were reviewed[125] regarding stay applications, 28 of those applications were

---

[124] Ibid 8 [1.8].

[125] '*VETiS* ', '*Institute of Training Pty Ltd*' (n 31), '*Technical Education Australia Pty Ltd*' (n 31) [104 - 105]; '*Trades College Australia Pty Ltd*' (n 31) [16], '*Australian Institute of Technical Training Pty Ltd*' (n 31) [53-54], '*Sher-E-Punjab Pty Ltd*' [104-106] (n 31), '*Business Institute of Australia Pty Ltd*' 11 (n 32) [30], '*Metro College of Technology Pty Ltd*' [34], '*Trades College Australia Pty Ltd*' [27-28] (n 31), '*Australian Trade Training and Assessment Pty Ltd*', '*Sydney Training Academy Pty Ltd*', '*Australian International College Pty Ltd*', *Australian Institute of Trades Pty Ltd as trustee for the Institute of Hotel Management Australia v Australian Skills Quality Authority* [2017] AATA 2912 (1 August 2017), *Oztech Trade Training College Pty Ltd v Australian Skills Quality Authority* [2018] AATA 3741 (9 October 2018),

LEGAL DECISION-MAKING UNDER THE
NATIONAL VOCATIONAL EDUCATION AND
TRAINING REGULATOR ACT 2011 (CTH): AN
INVESTIGATION INTO ACCESS TO MERITS
REVIEW

with legal representation where the hearing was conducted (on review of the reports) in an adversarial manner and in certain cases, in a Tribunal hearing room and frequently with cross-examination. The exact manner in which ASQA conducts itself during these hearings is consistent with the excerpt from the ARC

Sunrise Institute of Australia Pty Ltd v Australian Skills Quality Authority [2018] AATA 3935 (15 October 2018), *Real Training Outcomes v Australian Skills Quality Authority* [2018] AATA 4611 (18 December 2018), *Australian Vocational Learning Centre Pty Ltd v Australian Skills Quality Authority* [2018] AATA 4725 (21 December 2018), *Pacific Flight Services Pty Ltd v Australian Skills Quality Authority* (n 35) *Menzies Institute of Technology v Australian Skills Quality Authority* [2019] AATA 343 (12 February 2019), *Darwin Human Resource and Computer Academy Pty Ltd v Australian Skills Quality Authority* [2017] AATA 738 (24 May 2017), *Gurkhas Institute of Technology Pty Ltd trading as Gurkhas Institute of Technology ('Gurkhas') v Australian Skills Quality Authority* [2017] AATA 1018 (3 July 2017), *Skilled Education Australia Pty Limited v Australian Skills Quality Authority* [2019] AATA 317 (4 March 2019), *Chemcert Training Group v Australian Skills Quality Authority* [2019] AATA 313 (4 March 2019), *Daily Update Pty Ltd v Australian Skills Quality Authority* [2014] AATA 118 (6 March 2014), *Western Institute of Technology Pty Ltd v Australian Skills Quality Authority* [2018] AATA 94 (25 January 2018), *Elite Academy Australia Pty Ltd v Australian Skills Quality Authority* [2019] AATA 79 (5 February 2019), *BJSB Pty Ltd (t/a The Imperial College of Australia) v Australian Skills Quality Authority* [2019] AATA 1053 (30 May 2019), *Sunrise Institute of Australia Pty Ltd v Australian Skills Quality Authority* [2019] AATA 1131 (5 June 2019).

LEGAL DECISION-MAKING UNDER THE NATIONAL VOCATIONAL EDUCATION AND TRAINING REGULATOR ACT 2011 (CTH): AN INVESTIGATION INTO ACCESS TO MERITS REVIEW

Report finding above from the moment they are notified by the Tribunal that an application has been made.

The Tribunal notifies ASQA who immediately allocates the case to an ASQA lawyer who in each of these cases defends ASQA's original finding based on the previous legal decision that was made. One of the many reasons that this is problematic is because as a Commonwealth litigant, in accordance with the *Legal Services Directions 2017* (Cth), the Commonwealth's obligation to act as a model litigant, and the nature of that obligation are explicit.

Areas that are a frequent cause for concern in the Commonwealth's adherence to this obligation[126] include those areas highlighted below:

> The obligation to act as a model litigant requires
> that the Commonwealth and

---

[126] *Legal Services Directions 2017* (Cth) app B, s 2

LEGAL DECISION-MAKING UNDER THE NATIONAL VOCATIONAL EDUCATION AND TRAINING REGULATOR ACT 2011 (CTH): AN INVESTIGATION INTO ACCESS TO MERITS REVIEW

Commonwealth agencies act honestly **and fairly in handling claims and litigation** brought by or against the Commonwealth or a Commonwealth agency by:

(a) **dealing with claims promptly and not causing unnecessary delay in the handling of claims and litigation**

(aa) **making an early assessment of:**

    (i) **the Commonwealth's prospects of success in legal proceedings that may be brought against the Commonwealth; and**

    (ii) **the Commonwealth's potential liability in**

LEGAL DECISION-MAKING UNDER THE NATIONAL VOCATIONAL EDUCATION AND TRAINING REGULATOR ACT 2011 (CTH): AN INVESTIGATION INTO ACCESS TO MERITS REVIEW

claims against the

Commonwealth

(b) paying legitimate claims without litigation, including making partial settlements of claims or interim payments, where it is clear that liability is at least as much as the amount to be paid

(c) **acting consistently in the handling of claims and litigation**

(d) **endeavouring to avoid, prevent and limit the scope of legal proceedings wherever possible, including by giving consideration in all cases to alternative dispute resolution**

LEGAL DECISION-MAKING UNDER THE
NATIONAL VOCATIONAL EDUCATION AND
TRAINING REGULATOR ACT 2011 (CTH): AN
INVESTIGATION INTO ACCESS TO MERITS
REVIEW

before initiating legal
proceedings and by
participating in alternative
dispute resolution processes
where appropriate

(e) where it is not possible to
avoid litigation, keeping the
costs of litigation to a
minimum, including by:

(i) not requiring the other
party to prove a matter
which the
Commonwealth or the
agency knows to be true

(ii) not contesting liability if
the Commonwealth or the
agency knows that the

96

LEGAL DECISION-MAKING UNDER THE
NATIONAL VOCATIONAL EDUCATION AND
TRAINING REGULATOR ACT 2011 (CTH): AN
INVESTIGATION INTO ACCESS TO MERITS
REVIEW

dispute is really about
quantum

(iii) **monitoring the progress
of the litigation and
using methods that it
considers appropriate to
resolve the litigation,
including settlement
offers, payments into
court or alternative
dispute resolution, and**

(iv) ensuring that
arrangements are made so
that a person participating
in any settlement
negotiations on behalf of
the Commonwealth or a
Commonwealth agency can

LEGAL DECISION-MAKING UNDER THE NATIONAL VOCATIONAL EDUCATION AND TRAINING REGULATOR ACT 2011 (CTH): AN INVESTIGATION INTO ACCESS TO MERITS REVIEW

enter into a settlement of the claim or legal proceedings in the course of the negotiations

(f) **not taking advantage of a claimant who lacks the resources to litigate a legitimate claim**

(g) **not relying on technical defences unless the Commonwealth's or the agency's interests would be prejudiced by the failure to comply with a particular requirement**

(h) **not undertaking and pursuing appeals unless the Commonwealth or the**

LEGAL DECISION-MAKING UNDER THE NATIONAL VOCATIONAL EDUCATION AND TRAINING REGULATOR ACT 2011 (CTH): AN INVESTIGATION INTO ACCESS TO MERITS REVIEW

> **agency believes that it has reasonable prospects for success or the appeal is otherwise justified in the public interest, and**
>
> (i) **apologising where the Commonwealth or the agency is aware that it or its lawyers have acted wrongfully or improperly.**

Each of the areas highlighted is an area that has been a constant area of complaint from providers who have journeyed through the merits review process. Examples include that many providers do not get to finalise their application for merits review because the financial cost of fighting the application is or becomes too onerous. They do not often have sufficient funds; and very few, if any providers who have pursued and been successful in

LEGAL DECISION-MAKING UNDER THE NATIONAL VOCATIONAL EDUCATION AND TRAINING REGULATOR ACT 2011 (CTH): AN INVESTIGATION INTO ACCESS TO MERITS REVIEW

an appeals process against ASQA have for example received the apology referred to at (i). Every ASQA matter is managed at the Tribunal by an ASQA lawyer meaning that if the provider cannot afford a lawyer, they are required to self-represent making the process unfair and intimidatory.

On this basis, it would appear that the concerns of the ARC Report from 1995 (24 years ago) are resurfacing in today's Tribunals a factor briefly discussed in relation to the model litigant obligation.[127] Additional likenesses can be identified between the ARC Report and merits review proceedings in Australia in this area today however they are beyond the scope of this research.

One feature that is not so often discussed in relation to merits review in these hearings but often arises as a

---

[127] *Legal Services Directions 2017* (Cth) app B s 1 ("Model Litigant Rules").

LEGAL DECISION-MAKING UNDER THE NATIONAL VOCATIONAL EDUCATION AND TRAINING REGULATOR ACT 2011 (CTH): AN INVESTIGATION INTO ACCESS TO MERITS REVIEW

further challenge in this adversarial, costly and overly complex process is that while an NVR RTO can provide fresh evidence, so too can ASQA and it is becoming more and more frequent that it attempts to do so.

Either party is able to produce fresh evidence in merits review hearings to assist the Tribunal to ensure that the correct and preferable decision is made. It becomes problematic when the correct and preferable decision however is increased, and additional factors sought that were not initially presented to the provider as being a concern. Legal literature provides examples such as *New South Wales Thoroughbred Racing Board v Waterhouse* (2003) 56 NSWLR 691, 711, there is an example of this in case law related to VET and ASQA proceedings, that of *G Plus G Global Trading Pty Ltd v Australian Skills Quality Authority*[128] highlighting that 'everything is on the table'.

---

[128] *G Plus G Global Trading Pty Ltd v Australian Skills Quality Authority* [2013] AATA 698 (23 September 2013).

LEGAL DECISION-MAKING UNDER THE NATIONAL VOCATIONAL EDUCATION AND TRAINING REGULATOR ACT 2011 (CTH): AN INVESTIGATION INTO ACCESS TO MERITS REVIEW

ASQA often uses options available to it under the NVR Act[129] to obtain further evidence to improve their case at merits review.

Such options include the use of s 26 notices, s 62 requests and in more recent times, what is commonly known in the sector as 72-hour notices which effectively prevent an RTO from seeking a stay of the decision once it has been made. While the provider is battling to produce sufficient evidence to ensure support the Tribunal to make the correct and preferable decision regarding the legal decision that it was initially required to review, ASQA is often busy extending the basis for that legal decision by procuring additional reasons for the decision when the provider is least able to defend themselves appropriately.

---

[129] NVR Act.

LEGAL DECISION-MAKING UNDER THE NATIONAL VOCATIONAL EDUCATION AND TRAINING REGULATOR ACT 2011 (CTH): AN INVESTIGATION INTO ACCESS TO MERITS REVIEW

These issues are beyond the scope of this paper but are highlighted as they are tools that are frequently used by ASQA in this adversarial, costly and overly complex process. Considering the flawed foundation that these actions and legal decisions are based on, one must question whether the objectives of the NVR Act[130] are being upheld by the VET Regulator and how they can consistently claim to have complied with the Standards for VET Regulators.

It is important to consider 'The Obligation'[131] that ASQA has as a model litigant and the significant concerns being raised around the nature of this obligation,[132] particularly around the areas of:

- dealing with claims promptly and not causing unnecessary delay in the handling of claims and

---

[130] Ibid s 2A
[131] Model Litigant Rules (n 127) app B.
[132] Ibid app B s 2.

LEGAL DECISION-MAKING UNDER THE NATIONAL VOCATIONAL EDUCATION AND TRAINING REGULATOR ACT 2011 (CTH): AN INVESTIGATION INTO ACCESS TO MERITS REVIEW

litigation[133] (this extends to merits review proceedings);[134]

- not taking advantage of a claimant who lacks the resources to litigate a legitimate claim;[135]

- not undertaking and pursuing appeals unless the Commonwealth or the agency believes that it has reasonable prospects for success, or the appeal is otherwise justified in the public interest;[136] and

- apologising where the Commonwealth or the agency is aware that it or its lawyers have acted wrongfully or improperly.[137]

One of the biggest challenges in relation to the obligation being breached by ASQA is the manner in which a breach of any obligation needs to be notified.

---

[133] Ibid app B s 2(a).
[134] Ibid app B s 3.
[135] Ibid app B s 2(f).
[136] Ibid app B s 2(h).
[137] Ibid app B s 2(i).

LEGAL DECISION-MAKING UNDER THE NATIONAL VOCATIONAL EDUCATION AND TRAINING REGULATOR ACT 2011 (CTH): AN INVESTIGATION INTO ACCESS TO MERITS REVIEW

For legal practitioners and experts who practice in this field on a regular basis, there are other areas of concern around the obligation that are equally worthy of investigation although further investigation is beyond the scope of this paper.

Analysis of the stay applications referred to throughout this research appears to support the findings of this research.

This is especially with regards to the culture of ASQA,[138] how it manages merits review and the prospects of success[139] in opposing unfettered stay applications, or even stays with conditions applied that can be detrimental to the NVR RTO's ability to continue to access merits review.[140] Based on this review, it can be

---

[138] For example, at least 1 ASQA lawyer lists their wins on their professional social media profile.

[139] The prospects of success referred to in this statement are different to those referred to by Tribunal members when undertaking their discretionary powers.

[140] See '*VETiS Consulting Pty Ltd*' (n 31) and *Success Fast-Track Pty Ltd v*

LEGAL DECISION-MAKING UNDER THE NATIONAL VOCATIONAL EDUCATION AND TRAINING REGULATOR ACT 2011 (CTH): AN INVESTIGATION INTO ACCESS TO MERITS REVIEW

seen that a provider is more likely to have an application refused (15) than to have it granted (4) or granted with conditions (6). Three providers had their stay order revoked and 1 provider had their application for a variation of the stay order refused. Certain Tribunal members are more likely to refuse a stay than others; for example, Senior Member Puplick in Sydney (8 refusals v 2 grants), Senior Member Poljak in Sydney (5 refusals v 3 grants) and a provider is less likely to have a stay granted in Sydney than in Melbourne. Likewise, when an application is allocated to certain ASQA lawyers, a provider is more likely to have their application refused, for example, Ms McDermott (7 refusals), Mr Cox (4 refusals) and Messrs Grullemans and Lloyd 3 refusals each.

Australian Skills Quality Authority (n 35).

LEGAL DECISION-MAKING UNDER THE NATIONAL VOCATIONAL EDUCATION AND TRAINING REGULATOR ACT 2011 (CTH): AN INVESTIGATION INTO ACCESS TO MERITS REVIEW

Consideration of Stay Applications

Reference was made earlier to the prospects of success in seeking a stay of a decision from ASQA. When Tribunal Members consider making a stay order,[141] all members referred to the prospects of success as relevant factors that informed their decision. The prospects of success as seen in *Scott v Australian Securities and Investments Commission*[142] are well documented in case law and include a consideration of the:

- Prospects of success in the substantive hearing;
- The consequences for the applicant of the refusal of the stay;
- The public interest;
- The consequences for the Respondent in carrying out its functions depending on whether a stay was not granted or not;

---

[141] AAT Act s 41(2).
[142] *Anthony Scott v Australian Securities and Investment Commission* (2009) 51 AAR 114.

LEGAL DECISION-MAKING UNDER THE NATIONAL VOCATIONAL EDUCATION AND TRAINING REGULATOR ACT 2011 (CTH): AN INVESTIGATION INTO ACCESS TO MERITS REVIEW

- Whether the application for review would be rendered nugatory if a stay were not granted; and

- Any other relevant matters.

What is becoming more and more frequent during these stay applications is in order to demonstrate proper consideration of the prospects of success above, Tribunal Members are engaging in what is commonly referred to in the sector as a 'mini trial'.[143]

As stated in *Menzies Institute of Technology v Australian Skills Quality Authority*:

> The Tribunal acknowledges that in considering whether to grant a stay, it is not appropriate to undertake a full consideration of the merits of the substantive applications...However, the Tribunal considers that it is able to and that it is appropriate to take into account the information

---

[143] For example, see '*Gurkhas*' (n 125) [29].

and evidence presently available to form a general impression as to Menzies' prospects of success.[144]

In *Snook and Civil Aviation Safety Authority* [2008] AATA 861; (2008) 109 ALD 122 [21] referred to in *Sher-E-Punjab Pty Ltd v Australian Skills Quality Authority*, we see another quote that is often referred to in case law, 'It is well understood that in considering an applicant's prospects of success for the purposes of a stay application, it is not appropriate to conduct a preliminary trial of the issue'.[145]

While the scope of this paper is not to discuss in detail the prospects of success, there are 3 matters that are considered as part of the *'prospects of success'* being considered by Tribunal Members that must be

---

[144] *'Menzies Institute of Technology'* (n 125) [19-20].
[145] *'Sher-E-Punjab Pty Ltd'* (n 31) [27].

LEGAL DECISION-MAKING UNDER THE NATIONAL VOCATIONAL EDUCATION AND TRAINING REGULATOR ACT 2011 (CTH): AN INVESTIGATION INTO ACCESS TO MERITS REVIEW

addressed, at least by way of an overview or introduction to the issues. The first issue is in relation to the financial viability of the provider during the merits review process. The second issue is in relation to reputational damage of the RTO; and the third issue is in relation to the public interest.

LEGAL DECISION-MAKING UNDER THE
NATIONAL VOCATIONAL EDUCATION AND
TRAINING REGULATOR ACT 2011 (CTH): AN
INVESTIGATION INTO ACCESS TO MERITS
REVIEW

Financial Viability

One of the most common components of the *'prospects of success'* argument is whether the RTO has the financial capacity to survive if no stay is granted or if a stay is granted with conditions. Typical conditions that might be imposed on a stay order include no new enrolments, marketing and/or issuing of certification.

Each of these factors has a significant impact on the financial viability of a provider. Putting aside that the underpinning legal decision made by ASQA that led to the application may well be flawed, invalid and/or unreliable, there is an important issue that a provider must demonstrate; that of financial viability. An RTO must provide evidence that it has sufficient funds at its disposal so the substantive review will not be rendered nugatory because the provider has run out of money, and/or that the provider would not be able to sustain

LEGAL DECISION-MAKING UNDER THE NATIONAL VOCATIONAL EDUCATION AND TRAINING REGULATOR ACT 2011 (CTH): AN INVESTIGATION INTO ACCESS TO MERITS REVIEW

itself financially if a stay were refused. This in itself is a catch 22 situation due to the FVRAR.

There have been occasions where a Tribunal has deemed that the provider has sufficient funds available that the imposition of conditions to a stay order would not cause considerable negative impacts to the RTO. Equally, there have been situations where the Tribunal has identified that to impose a conditional stay on a provider might cause the RTO to become financially unviable. There are issues with both scenarios. By demonstrating that a provider would not be able to sustain itself in these circumstances or suggesting that there are sufficient funds available, the provider runs the risk of not being able to meet one of its registration requirements, the FVRAR referred to earlier.

LEGAL DECISION-MAKING UNDER THE NATIONAL VOCATIONAL EDUCATION AND TRAINING REGULATOR ACT 2011 (CTH): AN INVESTIGATION INTO ACCESS TO MERITS REVIEW

By falling foul of this in the process of trying to access merits review, the RTO is at risk of being issued with a new Notice because everything is on the table as discussed earlier and this would become new evidence.

The provision of financial evidence to support the prospects of success is thus inextricably linked to those circumstances where the Tribunal finds that the provider has sufficient funds available to sustain itself. As part of the consideration of financial viability prior to and at the stay hearing, the RTO provides a copy of all financials to ASQA and is often cross-examined on its contents.

In doing this, ASQA is then empowered to use those new opportunities for finding evidence by way of issuing new Notices[146] such as a section 26 or section 62 Notices or 72-hour Notices.

---

[146] NVR Act.

LEGAL DECISION-MAKING UNDER THE NATIONAL VOCATIONAL EDUCATION AND TRAINING REGULATOR ACT 2011 (CTH): AN INVESTIGATION INTO ACCESS TO MERITS REVIEW

Having supported many providers through the preparation of such evidence within the usually short timeframes required by the Notices, it is this writer's experience that it is almost impossible to gather all required evidence in the required timeframe.

Often requests for information are so cumbersome that it requires significant additional resources to accommodate them and at a significant cost that was never budgeted for. Timeframes are often unreasonable, usually dating back to the first day of the provider's registration (if it was registered by ASQA to begin with) or, alternatively, from 1 July 2011 when the VET Regulator was established for those who transitioned to ASQA upon its establishment.

It is also the writer's experience that the requests can also be accompanied by unexpected audits and monitoring visits.

LEGAL DECISION-MAKING UNDER THE NATIONAL VOCATIONAL EDUCATION AND TRAINING REGULATOR ACT 2011 (CTH): AN INVESTIGATION INTO ACCESS TO MERITS REVIEW

These additional circumstances are usually ways of generating more evidence and draining the financial resources of the provider before the substantive hearing forcing them to withdraw. In other cases,[147] the cost to the provider's ongoing financial viability of not obtaining an unfettered stay order is so significant that they are forced to withdraw and accept the decision by the Regulator.

---

[147] '*VETiS Consulting Services Pty Ltd*'(n 31), '*Success Fast-Track Pty Ltd*'(n 35).

LEGAL DECISION-MAKING UNDER THE NATIONAL VOCATIONAL EDUCATION AND TRAINING REGULATOR ACT 2011 (CTH): AN INVESTIGATION INTO ACCESS TO MERITS REVIEW

Reputational Damage

ASQA recently changed its approach to the notification of sanction decisions.[148] ASQA publishes decisions in accordance with ss 209 and 216 of the NVR Act. Section 209 of the NVR Act provides for the release of information to the public if the information 'would reasonably inform a person's choice to enrol as a VET student with a registered training organisation'. Section 216[149] provides for the publication of certain information on the national register[150]. ASQA revised its policy regarding the publication of regulatory decisions so that information about decisions is published soon after they have been made but before all avenues of appeal have been exhausted.

---

[148] As of 1 July 2016.

[149] NVR Act.

[150] The national register of Vocational Education and Training available online at <https://www.training.gov.au>.

LEGAL DECISION-MAKING UNDER THE NATIONAL VOCATIONAL EDUCATION AND TRAINING REGULATOR ACT 2011 (CTH): AN INVESTIGATION INTO ACCESS TO MERITS REVIEW

The details included on the decision table are significant[151] and remain on the ASQA website indefinitely. Considering there is evidence to question the basis upon which those legal decisions have been made, it is strongly recommended that this policy be reviewed. The impact of such information being published before any avenues of appeal have been exhausted is not only potentially damaging to the future viability of the provider, but also to the personal reputation of those individuals identified on the ASQA website. It is rare that a Tribunal acknowledges such impacts[152] although one recent case demonstrated this awareness is growing.[153]

---

[151] Provider name (legal entity and trading names), provider number, all Higher Managerial Agents of the provider are identified personally, the type of decision, details of the decision, date of the decision, effective date, the status of decision and the status of the review.

[152] *Greenfield Education Pty Ltd v Australian Skills Quality Authority* [2018] AATA 4210 (9 November 2018) [13].

[153] '*Business Institute of Australia Pty Ltd*' (n 32).

LEGAL DECISION-MAKING UNDER THE NATIONAL VOCATIONAL EDUCATION AND TRAINING REGULATOR ACT 2011 (CTH): AN INVESTIGATION INTO ACCESS TO MERITS REVIEW

The Public Interest

Much has been said within reported cases in relation to the public interest, indeed, it is ASQA's favourite argument[154] for a refusal of a stay order or to support a stay order that has crippling conditions attached. A good overview of how most Tribunal Members approach the consideration of *'the public interest'* in stay hearings relevant to the VET sector is best summarised in *Australian Vocational Learning Centre Pty Ltd v Australian Skills Quality Authority*:[155]

> In the view of the Tribunal, the public interest is best served by not allowing the Applicant to continue to operate, as it is, in a way which is non-compliant with the Standards and in the absence of immediate and effective remedial action having commenced.

---

[154] For example, see *'Western Institute of Technology Pty Ltd'* [21], *'Pacific Flight Services Pty Ltd'* 11 [38].
[155] *'Australian Vocational Learning Centre Pty Ltd'* (n 125) [40-42].

LEGAL DECISION-MAKING UNDER THE
NATIONAL VOCATIONAL EDUCATION AND
TRAINING REGULATOR ACT 2011 (CTH): AN
INVESTIGATION INTO ACCESS TO MERITS
REVIEW

Additional comments include '... the tribunal held that the public interest in having a registered provider meet the required standards and conditions laid down in legislation outweighed any disadvantage to an individual non-complying provider'.[156]

Further commentary that is often relied upon in Tribunal proceedings in relation to the public interest is that of Senior Member McCabe in *Metro College of Technology*:[157]

> But there is also the question of the public interest. The regulatory system was devised to protect consumers of these courses, and to protect the good name of Australian educational institutions overseas. Many students travel long distances from overseas [...] The regulatory

---

[156] Ibid [41].
[157] *Metro College of Technology Pty Ltd and Australian Skills Quality Authority* (Unreported).

regime assumes there is a public interest in ensuring these programs are properly run according to recognized(*sic*) standards. Failures to adhere to standards – particularly where those failures suggest systemic problems, poor judgment(*sic*) or an unwillingness to comply with the law – must be taken very seriously.

Considering the issues highlighted in this paper, it is imperative that the public interest is considered far beyond what Senior Member McCabe initially meant and that perhaps, it is in the public interest that these same issues should be considered with ASQA 'in the hot seat' as opposed to alleged non-complying RTOs. One can only ask the following questions…

What happens when, as has been demonstrated through this research, the very basis for legal decision-making 'in

LEGAL DECISION-MAKING UNDER THE NATIONAL VOCATIONAL EDUCATION AND TRAINING REGULATOR ACT 2011 (CTH): AN INVESTIGATION INTO ACCESS TO MERITS REVIEW

the public interest' is potentially erroneous and based on an unqualified foundation? Is that in the public interest? The more critical consideration for the public interest would be '*Are these decisions being made by ASQA legally sound*'?

The writer is confident that like the public, Tribunals have an expectation that the legal decisions that come before it are based on sound and valid legal reasoning and would concur that it is in the public interest that the VET regulator critically review its approach to legal decision making under the NVR Act before seeking further sanctions of this nature in a merits review process.

Senior Member Puplick stated that:

> Regulatory bodies are established, in part, to ensure that the public interest is protected in the areas of their competence and the Tribunal

LEGAL DECISION-MAKING UNDER THE NATIONAL VOCATIONAL EDUCATION AND TRAINING REGULATOR ACT 2011 (CTH): AN INVESTIGATION INTO ACCESS TO MERITS REVIEW

should be cautious about taking steps which may derogate from the protection of the public interest by failing to give due regard (although not unqualified deference) to their assessments in such matters.[158]

It is the contention of this paper that Puplick's comments could not have been more appropriate. While his intention was not meant to question the competence of the VET Regulator, it is suggested that his comments should now be considered in this regard, particularly given the substantial taxpayer dollars being absorbed by ASQA in this process.

---

[158] '*Australian Vocational Learning Centre Pty Ltd*' (n 125) [42].

LEGAL DECISION-MAKING UNDER THE NATIONAL VOCATIONAL EDUCATION AND TRAINING REGULATOR ACT 2011 (CTH): AN INVESTIGATION INTO ACCESS TO MERITS REVIEW

Conclusion and Recommendation

There are many issues not yet discussed that could also provide greater insight and transparency into a complex area of Australia's third largest export. The scope of this paper is not significant enough to consider other critical issues that are impacted by what is fast becoming a futile merits review process for this industry.

It is recommended that further research be undertaken in relation to those issues which include (but are not limited to):

- the impact on student visas;
- the impact on Australia's skills shortages;
- the differential approach to regulation between the public and private sector;
- the loss of technical expertise and educational legacy driven by regulatory burden;

LEGAL DECISION-MAKING UNDER THE
NATIONAL VOCATIONAL EDUCATION AND
TRAINING REGULATOR ACT 2011 (CTH): AN
INVESTIGATION INTO ACCESS TO MERITS
REVIEW

- the cost of compliance with a forever shifting bar;

- The personal impact that the issues discussed in this paper are experiencing including family breakdown, divorce, loss of family homes, bankruptcy, high unemployment and inability to find work subsequent to these decisions;

- Significant trauma; and

- The inability to recover costs or damages for wrongful decisions and the impacts that those erroneous legal decisions have had.

The few reviews that have been undertaken in the VET sector do little to open the can of worms that unravels when the issues described throughout this paper are raised publicly or privately. It is the writer's experience that many discuss them in private but very few will publicly share their views for fear of retaliation by the regulator. Yet, these issues are discussed frequently by

LEGAL DECISION-MAKING UNDER THE NATIONAL VOCATIONAL EDUCATION AND TRAINING REGULATOR ACT 2011 (CTH): AN INVESTIGATION INTO ACCESS TO MERITS REVIEW

the legal profession, at least those who work in this space on a regular basis.

Perhaps this paper will be the beginning of those discussions; a closer inspection of the legal decision-making process under the NVR Act may just prove to be in everyone's best interest, not just the public interest.

LEGAL DECISION-MAKING UNDER THE NATIONAL VOCATIONAL EDUCATION AND TRAINING REGULATOR ACT 2011 (CTH): AN INVESTIGATION INTO ACCESS TO MERITS REVIEW

Bonus Content

Commentary on Specific Cases

Australia Institute of Business and Technology (AIBT)

IMPORTANT NOTE:

Since this article was first published, this matter had been listed in the Federal Court of Australia to be heard on 5 June 2019. On the same day (5 June 2019), ASQA revoked its Decisions to Cancel AIBT's VET and CRICOS registrations. Subsequently, AIBT discontinued its action in the Federal Court of Australia.

Despite ASQA revoking their decisions, all of the information remains on the ASQA website. This action could cause irreparable damage to the reputation of the RTO and anyone associated with it.

LEGAL DECISION-MAKING UNDER THE NATIONAL VOCATIONAL EDUCATION AND TRAINING REGULATOR ACT 2011 (CTH): AN INVESTIGATION INTO ACCESS TO MERITS REVIEW

It portrays a negative image of an RTO that had the decisions revoked. As such, all details of this incident should have also been removed from the ASQA website.

This article (originally published on LinkedIn) was prompted by the recent media reports claiming *'another VET scandal that has emerged'* with the case regarding the Australia Institute of Business and Technology (AIBT) and the outcry regarding its HLT54115 Diploma of Nursing qualification. This article is not only about this provider however; the issues pertain to all those providers whose courses, both vocational and higher education have additional accreditation, regulatory, licensing or registration requirements.

LEGAL DECISION-MAKING UNDER THE NATIONAL VOCATIONAL EDUCATION AND TRAINING REGULATOR ACT 2011 (CTH): AN INVESTIGATION INTO ACCESS TO MERITS REVIEW

Disclaimer

Neither the author or RTO Doctor have any current association with AIBT, and the author provides comment on the issues based solely on publicly available information.

The author has no knowledge of the audit or operational processes that led to this situation.

LEGAL DECISION-MAKING UNDER THE NATIONAL VOCATIONAL EDUCATION AND TRAINING REGULATOR ACT 2011 (CTH): AN INVESTIGATION INTO ACCESS TO MERITS REVIEW

Discussion

Every course in the secondary school, vocational and higher education sectors has specific accreditation requirements and where these courses are being delivered across the different sectors, there are often further accreditation requirements that are required to be met (rightly or wrongly) and these can be confusing and poorly understood by those seeking to operate across multiple sectors.

The same can be said in some cases where the course or courses differ depending on the jurisdiction in which it is being delivered (*for a case in point, take anything to do with WHS/OHS in Victoria or Western Australia and the harmonisation of legislation as an example*). Then there is a whole other area of regulation which is deserving of attention, certainly more attention than it often receives by regulators, often, until it is too late.

LEGAL DECISION-MAKING UNDER THE NATIONAL VOCATIONAL EDUCATION AND TRAINING REGULATOR ACT 2011 (CTH): AN INVESTIGATION INTO ACCESS TO MERITS REVIEW

While this article could apply to other sectors such as the secondary school sector or the higher education sector and may at times make reference to a cross-sectoral approach to course registration, it will only deal with the vocational education and training (VET) sector. There are plenty of examples and cases where the issues this article seeks to address are just as valid and where these issues are equally prominent in these other sectors however, for the purpose of this article, they will not be explored.

LEGAL DECISION-MAKING UNDER THE NATIONAL VOCATIONAL EDUCATION AND TRAINING REGULATOR ACT 2011 (CTH): AN INVESTIGATION INTO ACCESS TO MERITS REVIEW

Shining the Light on Complex Registration Issues

The issue of additional course accreditation/registration requirements itself, receives very little attention on the website of the Australian Skills Quality Authority (ASQA) and certainly demands more respect and consideration than is provided. ASQA supposedly does have active MOU's with a range of regulators. It would appear however, that based on the writer's experience of rectification work and sanction management in the VET sector, that they do not use them as effectively and efficiently as they should. They are improperly utilised and considered tokenistic at best. For the purposes of substantiating this statement, you can take a look at just how critical this is to the sector by looking at a sample of the variety of courses in the VET sector that require some form of additional accreditation/registration/regulation.

LEGAL DECISION-MAKING UNDER THE
NATIONAL VOCATIONAL EDUCATION AND
TRAINING REGULATOR ACT 2011 (CTH): AN
INVESTIGATION INTO ACCESS TO MERITS
REVIEW

RTO Doctor prepared a list that is available by following the link https://www.linkedin.com/pulse/additional-accreditation-requirements-vet-sector-who-fault-bartlett/.

This is by no means a complete list of all of those courses in the VET sector (*or other sectors that integrate VET qualifications such as the secondary school sector delivering a range of Certificate courses to its year 11 and 12 students for example*) but it has been provided to demonstrate that for an area that is fraught with so much complexity, that ASQA provides so little guidance to providers, prospective providers and its own staff, including auditors, in the regulation of those courses.

This entire article arose from a report from the Australian Financial Review on 20 February 2019 "*Training Organisation Brighton Pacific has registration cancelled*" and subsequently on SBS "*International students*

LEGAL DECISION-MAKING UNDER THE NATIONAL VOCATIONAL EDUCATION AND TRAINING REGULATOR ACT 2011 (CTH): AN INVESTIGATION INTO ACCESS TO MERITS REVIEW

face uncertainty after regulator cancels AIBT's registration" on 22 February 2019 that quickly spread around the world. On LinkedIn there have also been comments and opinions shared.

For the case in discussion, the issue is around whether AIBT is solely to blame for the alleged consumer nightmare and international disgrace that yet again haunts the VET sector in Australia. It is the writer's experience, based on a review of the national media and social media that many people have been quick to point the finger at AIBT – including the National VET Regulator who has suddenly taken an opportunistic moment to advance the sanction imposed and it would appear, is under appeal.

Yet if one understands the regulatory space and accreditation requirements of the VET sector, as well as ANMAC's accreditation requirements, we soon come to

LEGAL DECISION-MAKING UNDER THE NATIONAL VOCATIONAL EDUCATION AND TRAINING REGULATOR ACT 2011 (CTH): AN INVESTIGATION INTO ACCESS TO MERITS REVIEW

realise that the National VET Regulator actually facilitated the current position and that they are just as much to blame for the current displacement of thousands of international students in Australia and overseas as AIBT allegedly is, if not more.

LEGAL DECISION-MAKING UNDER THE
NATIONAL VOCATIONAL EDUCATION AND
TRAINING REGULATOR ACT 2011 (CTH): AN
INVESTIGATION INTO ACCESS TO MERITS
REVIEW

The VET Legislative Framework

Firstly, the legislative basis for the National VET
Regulator and the Standards that they regulate, as well as
the Standards under which the National VET Regulator
must perform its functions, the *National Vocational
Education and Training Regulator Act 2011* (NVR Act). The
purpose of the NVR Act is captured below at s 2A:

LEGAL DECISION-MAKING UNDER THE NATIONAL VOCATIONAL EDUCATION AND TRAINING REGULATOR ACT 2011 (CTH): AN INVESTIGATION INTO ACCESS TO MERITS REVIEW

this Act.

2A Objects

The objects of this Act are:

(a) to provide for national consistency in the regulation of vocational education and training (*VET*); and

(b) to regulate VET using:

  (i) a standards–based quality framework; and

  (ii) risk assessments, where appropriate; and

(c) to protect and enhance:

  (i) quality, flexibility and innovation in VET; and

  (ii) Australia's reputation for VET nationally and internationally; and

(d) to provide a regulatory framework that encourages and promotes a VET system that is appropriate to meet Australia's social and economic needs for a highly educated and skilled population; and

(e) to protect students undertaking, or proposing to undertake, Australian VET by ensuring the provision of quality VET; and

(f) to facilitate access to accurate information relating to the quality of VET.

Note 1: The standards–based quality framework mentioned in paragraph (b) consists of instruments made by the Ministerial Council, the Minister or the National VET Regulator.

Note 2: These objects are subject to the constitutional basis for this Act (see Division 3).

https://www.legislation.gov.au/Details/C2017C00245

Under s 22 of the NVR Act, a VET provider or Registered Training Organisation (RTO) must comply with the VET Quality Framework which includes

136

LEGAL DECISION-MAKING UNDER THE
NATIONAL VOCATIONAL EDUCATION AND
TRAINING REGULATOR ACT 2011 (CTH): AN
INVESTIGATION INTO ACCESS TO MERITS
REVIEW

the *Standards for Registered Training Organisations (RTOs) 2015* (Standards for RTOs 2015):

22 Condition—compliance with the VET Quality Framework

(1) An NVR registered training organisation must comply with the Standards for NVR Registered Training Organisations.

(1A) An NVR registered training organisation must comply with the Quality Standards.

(2) An NVR registered training organisation must comply with the Australian Qualifications Framework.

(3) An NVR registered training organisation must comply with the Data Provision Requirements.

https://www.legislation.gov.au/Details/C2017C00245

Under s 35(1), the National VET Regulator is provided with authority to conduct audits to ensure compliance with the Standards for RTOs 2015:

LEGAL DECISION-MAKING UNDER THE NATIONAL VOCATIONAL EDUCATION AND TRAINING REGULATOR ACT 2011 (CTH): AN INVESTIGATION INTO ACCESS TO MERITS REVIEW

Division 3—Ensuring compliance with the VET Quality Framework

Subdivision A—Audits

35 Audits

(1) The National VET Regulator may, at any time, conduct a compliance audit of an NVR registered training organisation's operations to assess whether the organisation continues to comply with this Act or the VET Quality Framework.

(2) The National VET Regulator may also review or examine any aspect of an NVR registered training organisation's operations to determine any systemic issues relating to the quality of vocational education and training.

https://www.legislation.gov.au/Details/C2017C00245

The National VET Regulator is established by the NVR Act 2011 under s 155:

LEGAL DECISION-MAKING UNDER THE NATIONAL VOCATIONAL EDUCATION AND TRAINING REGULATOR ACT 2011 (CTH): AN INVESTIGATION INTO ACCESS TO MERITS REVIEW

Part 7—National Vocational Education and Training Regulator

Division 1—Establishment, functions and powers of Regulator

155 Establishment

(1) The National Vocational Education and Training Regulator (*National VET Regulator*) is established by this section.

(2) The National VET Regulator may also be known by a name specified in the regulations.

(3) Each State and Territory Education Minister must be consulted if the National VET Regulator is to be abolished.

https://www.legislation.gov.au/Details/C2017C00245

The National VET Regulator's functions are specified at

s 157, a snapshot is captured below:

LEGAL DECISION-MAKING UNDER THE NATIONAL VOCATIONAL EDUCATION AND TRAINING REGULATOR ACT 2011 (CTH): AN INVESTIGATION INTO ACCESS TO MERITS REVIEW

157 Functions of the National VET Regulator

(1) The National VET Regulator has the following functions:

(a) to register an organisation as an NVR registered training organisation;

(b) to accredit courses that may be offered and/or provided by registered training organisations;

(c) to carry out compliance audits of NVR registered training organisations;

(d) to promote, and encourage the continuous improvement of, a registered training organisation's capacity to provide a VET course or part of a VET course;

(e) if requested to do so by the Minister, or on the Regulator's own initiative, to advise and make recommendations to the Minister on matters relating to vocational education and training;

(f) if requested to do so, in writing, by the Education Minister for a State or Territory, or on the Regulator's own initiative, to advise and make recommendations to the Education Minister for the State or Territory on specific matters relating to vocational education and training in the State or Territory;

(g) if requested to do so, in writing, by the Chair of the Ministerial Council, or on the Regulator's own initiative, to advise and make recommendations to the Ministerial Council on general matters relating to vocational education and training in all jurisdictions;

(h) to collect, analyse, interpret and disseminate information about vocational education and training;

(i) to publish performance information, of a kind prescribed by the regulations, relating to NVR registered training organisations;

(j) to conduct training programs relating to the regulation of registered training organisations and/or the accreditation of courses;

(k) to enter into arrangements with occupational licensing bodies, other industry bodies, or both, for the purpose of ensuring compliance by NVR registered training organisations with this Act;

(l) to cooperate with a regulatory authority of another country that has responsibility relating to the quality or regulation of vocational education and training for all, or part, of the country;

(m) to develop relationships with its counterparts in other countries;

(n) to develop key performance indicators, to be agreed by the Minister, against which the Regulator's performance can be assessed each financial year;

(o) to develop service standards that the Regulator must meet in performing its functions;

(p) any other function relating to vocational education and training that is set out in a legislative instrument made by the Minister;

(q) such other functions as are conferred on the Regulator by or under:

(i) this Act; or

(ii) the *Education Services for Overseas Students Act 2000* or any other law of the Commonwealth;

LEGAL DECISION-MAKING UNDER THE
NATIONAL VOCATIONAL EDUCATION AND
TRAINING REGULATOR ACT 2011 (CTH): AN
INVESTIGATION INTO ACCESS TO MERITS
REVIEW

While s 225(1) of the NVR Act provides for the delegation of these responsibilities to occupational licensing bodies and industry bodies, it is not the case with AIBT's situation.

225 Delegation by the National VET Regulator—occupational licensing bodies and other industry bodies

(1) The National VET Regulator may, by writing, delegate all or any of the Regulator's functions and powers to an occupational licensing body or other industry body (other than one covered by section 224) that deals with, or has an interest in, matters relating to vocational education and training.

(2) A delegate under subsection (1) must comply with any written directions of the National VET Regulator.

https://www.legislation.gov.au/Details/C2017C00245

It is also not my experience that this occurs and judging by the ASQA website in relation to occupational

LEGAL DECISION-MAKING UNDER THE NATIONAL VOCATIONAL EDUCATION AND TRAINING REGULATOR ACT 2011 (CTH): AN INVESTIGATION INTO ACCESS TO MERITS REVIEW

licensing, ASQA's practice is inconsistent with this provision also:

Where licensing requirements differ from the requirements of the training package, RTOs must ensure that all aspects of the training package are met. Licensing requirements should be seen as additional to the training package requirements.

Sometimes, and this is not a matter for this article but may be addressed in a separate article in the future, this approach taken by the National VET Regulator can also lead to situations whereby complying with the relevant training package, the provider (*or student in complying with the requirements for valid assessment*) will potentially be in

LEGAL DECISION-MAKING UNDER THE NATIONAL VOCATIONAL EDUCATION AND TRAINING REGULATOR ACT 2011 (CTH): AN INVESTIGATION INTO ACCESS TO MERITS REVIEW

breach of other legislation due to poorly and inappropriately developed training packages.

LEGAL DECISION-MAKING UNDER THE
NATIONAL VOCATIONAL EDUCATION AND
TRAINING REGULATOR ACT 2011 (CTH): AN
INVESTIGATION INTO ACCESS TO MERITS
REVIEW

ASQA's requirements for registration of courses

ASQA is very clear in its position for a training provider to register a course on its scope of registration. For new and/or intending providers ASQA's website provides the following:

Understand the requirements for registration

If you are considering registration with ASQA, you must be prepared to meet the following requirements for registration:

- compliance with all components of the Vocational Education and Training (VET) Quality Framework:
    - Standards for Registered Training Organisations (RTOs) 2015
    - Australian Qualifications Framework
    - Fit and Proper Person Requirements
    - Financial Viability Risk Assessment Requirements 2011
    - Data Provision Requirements 2012.
- cooperation with ASQA—including compliance with general directions and cooperation with compliance monitoring activity
- payment of fees and charges associated with registration
- registration of courses on the Commonwealth Register of Institutions and Courses for Overseas Students (CRICOS) to offer those courses to overseas students on student visas
- additional requirements for RTOs offering VET courses with additional licensing requirements
- registration for at least two years before applying to deliver qualifications or assessor skill sets from the Training and Education Training Package.

LEGAL DECISION-MAKING UNDER THE NATIONAL VOCATIONAL EDUCATION AND TRAINING REGULATOR ACT 2011 (CTH): AN INVESTIGATION INTO ACCESS TO MERITS REVIEW

https://www.asqa.gov.au/vet-registration/understand-requirements-registration

The compliance assessment of this registration provision is against a legislative instrument called the *Standards for Registered Training Organisations (RTOs) 2015.*

The assessment is undertaken by the National VET Regulator under a different legislative instrument called the *Standards for VET Regulators 2015.* Both of these legislative instruments are given power through the *National Vocational Education and Training Regulator Act 2011.*

The relevant sections of the *Standards for Registered Training Organisations (RTOs) 2015* are predominantly around clause 1.8 and clause 8.5, although arguably, all clauses of the *Standards for Registered Training Organisations (RTOs) 2015* apply to each prospective and enrolled or certified student impacted by this situation.

LEGAL DECISION-MAKING UNDER THE NATIONAL VOCATIONAL EDUCATION AND TRAINING REGULATOR ACT 2011 (CTH): AN INVESTIGATION INTO ACCESS TO MERITS REVIEW

Assessment

1.8. The RTO implements an assessment system that ensures that assessment (including recognition of prior learning):

    a)   complies with the assessment requirements of the relevant training package or VET accredited course; and

    b)   is conducted in accordance with the Principles of Assessment contained in Table 1.8-1 and the Rules of Evidence contained in Table 1.8-2.

LEGAL DECISION-MAKING UNDER THE NATIONAL VOCATIONAL EDUCATION AND TRAINING REGULATOR ACT 2011 (CTH): AN INVESTIGATION INTO ACCESS TO MERITS REVIEW

Table 1.8-1: Principles of Assessment

Fairness	The individual learner's needs are considered in the assessment process.
	Where appropriate, reasonable adjustments are applied by the RTO to take into account the individual learner's needs.
	The RTO informs the learner about the assessment process, and provides the learner with the opportunity to challenge the result of the assessment and be reassessed if necessary.
Flexibility	Assessment is flexible to the individual learner by:
	• reflecting the learner's needs;
	• assessing competencies held by the learner no matter how or where they have been acquired; and
	• drawing from a range of assessment methods and using those that are appropriate to the context, the unit of competency and associated assessment requirements, and the individual.
Validity	Any assessment decision of the RTO is justified, based on the evidence of performance of the individual learner.
	Validity requires:
	• assessment against the unit/s of competency and the associated assessment requirements covers the broad range of skills and knowledge that are essential to competent performance;
	• assessment of knowledge and skills is integrated with their practical application;
	• assessment to be based on evidence that demonstrates that a learner could demonstrate these skills and knowledge in other similar situations; and
	• judgement of competence is based on evidence of learner performance that is aligned to the unit/s of competency and associated assessment requirements.
Reliability	Evidence presented for assessment is consistently interpreted and assessment results are comparable irrespective of the assessor conducting the assessment.

8.5. The RTO complies with Commonwealth, State and Territory legislation and regulatory requirements relevant to its operations.

LEGAL DECISION-MAKING UNDER THE NATIONAL VOCATIONAL EDUCATION AND TRAINING REGULATOR ACT 2011 (CTH): AN INVESTIGATION INTO ACCESS TO MERITS REVIEW

In the case of HLT54115 Diploma of Nursing, the qualification description on the national register of VET Training.Gov.Au is explicit about the requirements for registration:

Qualification Description

This qualification reflects the role of an enrolled nurse working under supervision of a registered nurse. This qualification covers the application of skills and knowledge required to provide nursing care for people across the health sector. A lifespan approach should underpin this qualification with relevant competencies that relate to the different stages of life identified within the units.

A graduate from a Diploma of Nursing program approved by the Nursing and Midwifery Board of Australia (NMBA) is able to apply for registration with the NMBA as an enrolled nurse. Further information on registration is available at www.nursingmidwiferyboard.gov.au

Note that the scope of practice for enrolled nurses is determined by state and territory legislative requirements and the policies and procedures of the employing organisation. Users of this qualification must refer to those instruments in the development of training and assessment strategies.

https://training.gov.au/Training/Details/HLT54115

The ASQA website, as lacking as it is on information regarding the issue of additional accreditation and registration requirements, is also explicit regarding nursing programs:

LEGAL DECISION-MAKING UNDER THE NATIONAL VOCATIONAL EDUCATION AND TRAINING REGULATOR ACT 2011 (CTH): AN INVESTIGATION INTO ACCESS TO MERITS REVIEW

Nominated industry authority arrangements

The following industry sectors are listed as guidance only. Evidence of approval from the relevant government agency/industry body will be required with a registration application.

Industry area	Training product	Application type	Industry authority	Application requirements
Health	HLT54115 Diploma of Nursing	NVR Act*: • Initial registration • Renewal of registration • Addition to scope ESOS Act**: • Initial registration • Renewal of registration • Addition of course	Australian Nursing and Midwifery Accreditation Council (ANMAC)	An application for registration for HLT54115 will only be considered complete if supported by evidence confirming that the applicant organisation has ANMAC accreditation. See the ANMAC website's section on program accreditation. If approved, the organisation must maintain ANMAC accreditation for its entire period of registration for HLT54115.

https://www.asqa.gov.au/vet-registration/understand-requirements-registration/other-licensing-and-registration-requirements

LEGAL DECISION-MAKING UNDER THE NATIONAL VOCATIONAL EDUCATION AND TRAINING REGULATOR ACT 2011 (CTH): AN INVESTIGATION INTO ACCESS TO MERITS REVIEW

The Nursing and Midwifery Board of Australia (NMBA) website, described on the qualification descriptor is also clear about the requirements for accreditation of the relevant course:

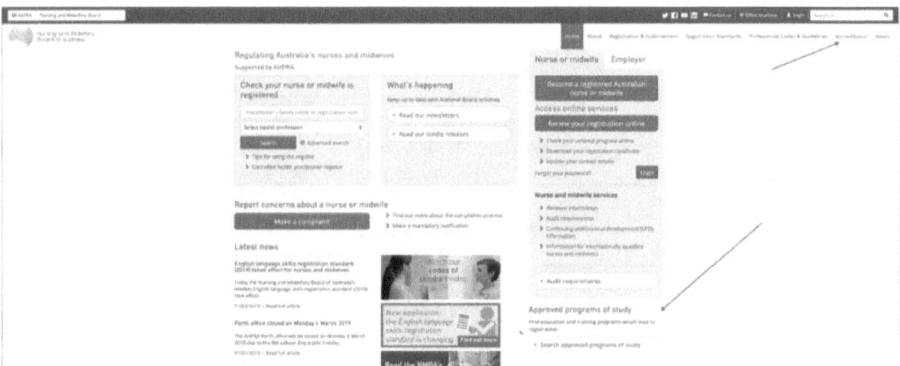

https://www.nursingmidwiferyboard.gov.au/

LEGAL DECISION-MAKING UNDER THE NATIONAL VOCATIONAL EDUCATION AND TRAINING REGULATOR ACT 2011 (CTH): AN INVESTIGATION INTO ACCESS TO MERITS REVIEW

https://www.nursingmidwiferyboard.gov.au/Accreditati on.aspx

The Australian Nursing and Midwifery Accreditation Council (ANMAC) is also very explicit about its course accreditation and program standards and the approval of programs that will lead to registration:

LEGAL DECISION-MAKING UNDER THE NATIONAL VOCATIONAL EDUCATION AND TRAINING REGULATOR ACT 2011 (CTH): AN INVESTIGATION INTO ACCESS TO MERITS REVIEW

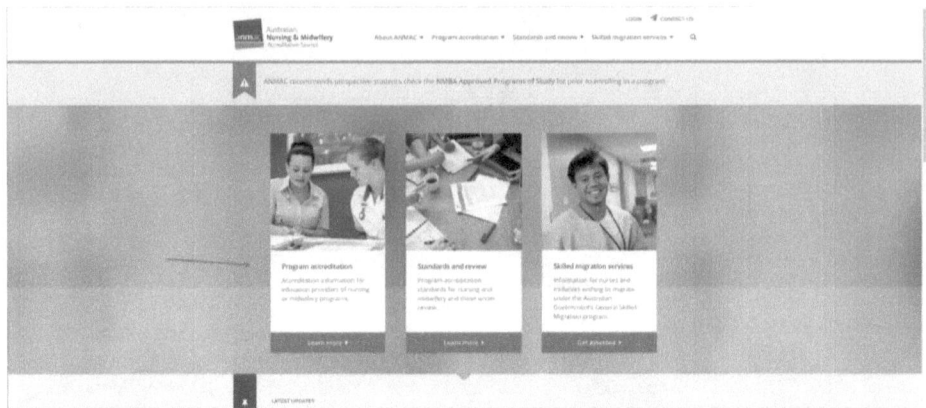

https://www.anmac.org.au/

LEGAL DECISION-MAKING UNDER THE NATIONAL VOCATIONAL EDUCATION AND TRAINING REGULATOR ACT 2011 (CTH): AN INVESTIGATION INTO ACCESS TO MERITS REVIEW

https://www.anmac.org.au/program-accreditation

The ANMAC webpage relevant to the Enrolled Nursing program is also very explicit about the minimum requirements to be met by vocational education and training providers:

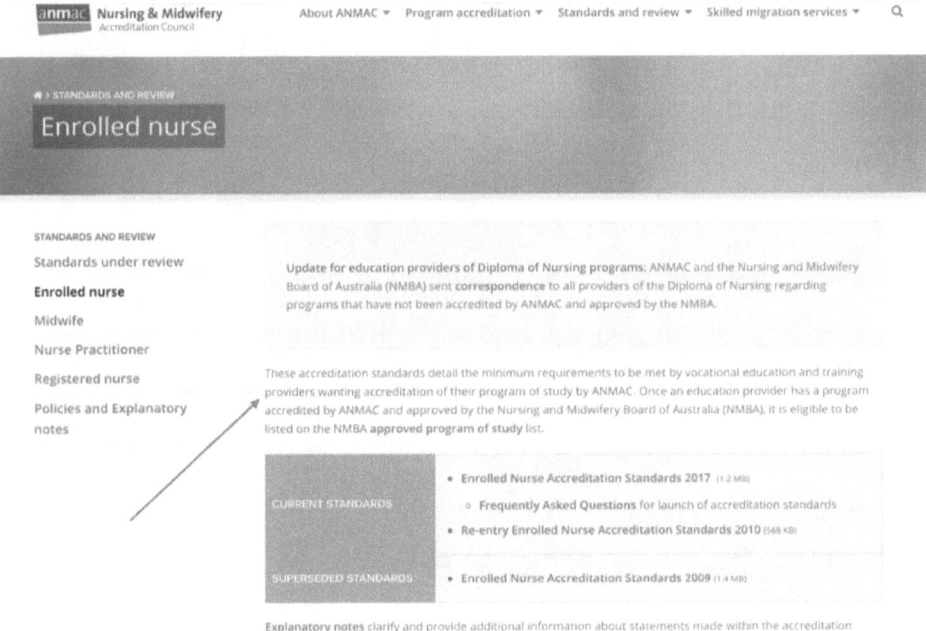

LEGAL DECISION-MAKING UNDER THE NATIONAL VOCATIONAL EDUCATION AND TRAINING REGULATOR ACT 2011 (CTH): AN INVESTIGATION INTO ACCESS TO MERITS REVIEW

https://www.anmac.org.au/standards-and-review/enrolled-nurse

Based on these screenshots, it is very clear to even the most uninitiated observer that there is a mandatory requirement for any HLT54115 Diploma of Nursing course to be accredited by the ANMAC if the graduate of the course is to be eligible for registration with the NMBA and thus employable as an enrolled nurse in Australia.

Therefore, it would seem incumbent upon the regulator to ensure that the provider / course has had the relevant approval from the ANMAC at the time of risk review and audit as per the screenshots from the Standards for RTOs 2015 previously. This should occur either at the time of registration or adding the qualification to their scope of registration if an already existing provider.

LEGAL DECISION-MAKING UNDER THE NATIONAL VOCATIONAL EDUCATION AND TRAINING REGULATOR ACT 2011 (CTH): AN INVESTIGATION INTO ACCESS TO MERITS REVIEW

LEGAL DECISION-MAKING UNDER THE
NATIONAL VOCATIONAL EDUCATION AND
TRAINING REGULATOR ACT 2011 (CTH): AN
INVESTIGATION INTO ACCESS TO MERITS
REVIEW

Standards for VET Regulators 2015

What is clear in the following screenshots is that the National VET Regulator had certain mandatory performance obligations under its own Standards to ensure that these requirements were met. Below is a range of key sections from the legislation that provides the basis for the performance of the National VET Regulator.

LEGAL DECISION-MAKING UNDER THE NATIONAL VOCATIONAL EDUCATION AND TRAINING REGULATOR ACT 2011 (CTH): AN INVESTIGATION INTO ACCESS TO MERITS REVIEW

Purpose

The purpose of these Standards is to ensure:

- the integrity of nationally recognised training by regulating RTOs and VET accredited courses using a risk-based approach that is consistent, effective, proportional, responsive and transparent;
- consistency in the VET Regulator's implementation and interpretation of the RTO Standards and Standards for VET Accredited Courses; and
- the accountability and transparency of the VET Regulator in undertaking its regulatory functions.

Context:

The Standards require a risk-based approach to the regulation of RTOs that is informed by assessments of RTO compliance with the Standards for RTOs on an ongoing basis. This risk management approach enables VET Regulators to more actively and regularly apply strategies to reduce the regulatory burden for high-performing RTOs with a history of strong compliance and to increase regulatory action for those RTOs considered as higher risk. This is achieved through regulatory strategies that can include:

- an active and dynamic risk assessment process that is based on compliance history, performance data, outcomes of complaints against RTOs, and industry and learner intelligence;

- varying the type and regularity of audits, based on risk assessments;

- recognising and not duplicating the decisions of other relevant regulators; and

- delegating regulatory powers to low-risk RTOs, such as the ability to amend their scope of registration.

Regulation must be sufficient to assure the quality outcomes of the Standards for RTOs and the Standards for VET Accredited Courses, with VET Regulators using the strength of their regulatory tools to deter non-compliance. The regulatory approach should engender self-evaluation and improvement within RTOs in a way that makes regulation valued for what it contributes to RTOs, industry stakeholders and learners.

Structure

These Standards consist of six Standards. Under each Standard is a set of Clauses. To comply with a Standard, the VET Regulator must meet each Clause.

Definitions

The glossary at the beginning of these Standards defines certain words and expressions which have specific meaning in these Standards.

LEGAL DECISION-MAKING UNDER THE NATIONAL VOCATIONAL EDUCATION AND TRAINING REGULATOR ACT 2011 (CTH): AN INVESTIGATION INTO ACCESS TO MERITS REVIEW

PART 2 – Regulator Standards

Standard 1.   The VET Regulator effectively and efficiently regulates RTOs.

Context:

The quality of the regulation of RTOs is crucial to ensuring the credibility of the VET system. This is achieved through effective and efficient processes and practices that are fair, risk-based, transparent, responsive, consistent, and meet legislative requirements.

In addition to using a risk-based approach the VET Regulator has:

- *robust and transparent decision making processes;*
- *auditors who meet national competency requirements; and*
- *procedures and practices in place to promote consistency in auditor judgements.*

To be compliant with Standard 1 the VET Regulator must meet the following:

1.1. The VET Regulator only grants registration or renews registration where it has determined that the person complies with the Standards for RTOs.

1.2. The VET Regulator conducts an audit of the RTO within two years of the RTO first being registered.

1.3. In enforcing the Standards for RTOs, the VET Regulator:

   a) adopts a risk-based approach to regulation consistent with the risk assessment framework;

   b) encourages RTOs to improve their performance;

   c) ensures that its actions taken to mitigate risk of, or respond to, non-compliance are responsive and proportionate; and

   d) makes publically available information about how it assesses risk and arrives at risk ratings.

1.4. The VET Regulator provides general education and guidance materials to RTOs to assist them to comply with the Standards for RTOs.

1.5. The VET Regulator only grants an application to add any AQF qualification or assessor skill set from the Training and Education Training Package (or its successor) to the RTO's scope of registration, if an RTO has:

   a) held registration for at least two years continuously at the time of adding the qualification and/or skill set to scope; and

   b) from 1 January 2016, undergone an independent validation of its assessment system, tools, processes and outcomes in accordance with the requirements contained in the Standards for RTOs.

1.6. The VET Regulator ensures that:

   a) an RTO's scope of registration is not extended while instances of non-compliance remain outstanding unless action to address all relevant non-compliance is being progressed to the satisfaction of the VET Regulator;

   b) subject to Clause 1.7, where a training product is superseded, the VET Regulator removes the training product from the RTO's current scope of registration one year from the date the replacement training product was released on the National Register;

LEGAL DECISION-MAKING UNDER THE
NATIONAL VOCATIONAL EDUCATION AND
TRAINING REGULATOR ACT 2011 (CTH): AN
INVESTIGATION INTO ACCESS TO MERITS
REVIEW

As can be seen from the purpose of this legislation, the National VET Regulator is responsible for ensuring that through its regulation of training providers and nationally recognised training that the integrity of the Australian VET sector is maintained. What we can see through this article is that the National VET Regulator has failed in this instance and has actually facilitated the compromise of integrity. It is also required to recognise and not duplicate the decisions of other relevant regulators, in this case, the ANMAC, and regulation must be consistent with the Standards for RTOs 2015 (in this case).

In the second screenshot, we see the critical context of Standard 1 of the *Standards for VET Regulators 2015*. In clause 1.1, it is confirmed that the regulator must only

LEGAL DECISION-MAKING UNDER THE NATIONAL VOCATIONAL EDUCATION AND TRAINING REGULATOR ACT 2011 (CTH): AN INVESTIGATION INTO ACCESS TO MERITS REVIEW

grant registration where the training provider meets the Standards for RTOs 2015. It is also important to note clause 1.2, that the National VET Regulator undertakes an audit within 2 years of registration.

I have no knowledge of whether audits were, or were not conducted within the first 2 years but this is what I do know from publicly available information:

1. AIBT was initially registered on 4 May 2015 for a period of 7 years;

2. On 27 May 2017 (just over 2 years later), they had HLT54115 Diploma of Nursing added to their scope of registration;

3. AIBT have several other qualifications on their scope of registration that have additional accreditation/registration requirements including for example:

LEGAL DECISION-MAKING UNDER THE NATIONAL VOCATIONAL EDUCATION AND TRAINING REGULATOR ACT 2011 (CTH): AN INVESTIGATION INTO ACCESS TO MERITS REVIEW

(a) AVI30316 Certificate III in Aviation (Remote Pilot – Visual Line of Sight);

(b) AVI50616 Diploma of Aviation (Aviation Management);

(c) Accounting qualifications which potentially have accreditation/registration requirements;

(d) HLT52015 Diploma of Remedial Massage (*provided graduates wish to be eligible for health rebates for their prospective clients, otherwise they are likely to be unemployable*);

(e) UEE20111 Certificate II in Split Air Conditioning and Heat-Pump Systems;

(f) UEE32211 Certificate III in Air-conditioning and Refrigeration;

(g) A range of other electrical and air conditioning qualifications;

(h) All of the qualifications listed above are all registered on CRICOS (Commonwealth

LEGAL DECISION-MAKING UNDER THE NATIONAL VOCATIONAL EDUCATION AND TRAINING REGULATOR ACT 2011 (CTH): AN INVESTIGATION INTO ACCESS TO MERITS REVIEW

Register of Institutions and Course for Overseas Students), an issue that will make this entire case with AIBT even more difficult to comprehend.

4.   All of those qualifications in the previous point had been added to the scope of registration within that 2-year period. So, either there were no audits conducted relevant to the HLT54115 Diploma of Nursing, those audits did not satisfy the requirement of the *Standards for VET Regulators 2015 or the Standards for RTOs 2015*, or some mysterious issue that I cannot possibly fathom has arisen.

We can also see in the following screenshot, an equally critical requirement for the national regulator to engage with other regulators as appropriate:

LEGAL DECISION-MAKING UNDER THE NATIONAL VOCATIONAL EDUCATION AND TRAINING REGULATOR ACT 2011 (CTH): AN INVESTIGATION INTO ACCESS TO MERITS REVIEW

Standards for VET Regulators 2015
Compilation No.1   Compilation Date: 14/04/2017   9

Authorised Version F2017C00444 registered 06/06/2017

c) where an AQF qualification is no longer current and is not superseded, the VET Regulator removes the qualification from the RTO's current scope of registration two years from the date the qualification was removed or deleted from the National Register; and

d) where a skill set, unit of competency, accredited short course or module is no longer current and has not been superseded, the VET Regulator removes the skill set, unit of competency, accredited short course or module from the RTO's current scope of registration one year from the date the skill set, unit of competency, accredited short course or module was removed or deleted from the National Register.

1.7. The requirements specified in Clause 1.6.b) do not apply where a training package requires delivery of a superseded unit of competency.

1.8. The VET Regulator implements a risk-based approach to managing changes to RTO ownership or management, and publishes clear information about its processes and requirements.

1.9. The VET Regulator ensures that its auditors:

a) adopt contemporary best practice auditing approaches; and

b) exercise their judgement in a manner which maximises consistent interpretation of the Standards for RTOs, audit practice and findings across audits; and

c) from 1 January 2016, meet the national competency requirements for auditors specified in Schedule 1.

1.10. The VET Regulator makes decisions in a manner consistent with the principles of natural justice and procedural fairness.

1.11. In conducting industry reviews and projects, the VET Regulator engages with other regulators as appropriate, including industry regulators, and with industry.

It is unclear how the National VET Regulator satisfied these crucial legislative requirements in approving the

LEGAL DECISION-MAKING UNDER THE NATIONAL VOCATIONAL EDUCATION AND TRAINING REGULATOR ACT 2011 (CTH): AN INVESTIGATION INTO ACCESS TO MERITS REVIEW

application for AIBT to add HLT54115 Diploma of Nursing to its scope of registration if the situation is as claimed in the media reports (as discussed earlier) and by ASQA. Instead, what this blatantly demonstrates is a complete disregard for and breach of the very legislation that supports ASQA's decision-making powers.

For the domestic only providers who deliver the HLT54115 Diploma of Nursing, this is where the regulatory interface should end; with the program having been endorsed and accredited by the ANMAC and ASQA, they should now be free to deliver a program that satisfies the requirements of the NMBA. However, it is sadly very rarely followed.

As a Consultant, I often receive enquiries from providers who have had their application approved by ASQA and they are applying for ANMAC approval or

LEGAL DECISION-MAKING UNDER THE NATIONAL VOCATIONAL EDUCATION AND TRAINING REGULATOR ACT 2011 (CTH): AN INVESTIGATION INTO ACCESS TO MERITS REVIEW

worse, they have the course on their scope of registration and were oblivious to the requirements of ANMAC. This however was not the case for AIBT. AIBT, as a CRICOS provider, and a CRICOS provider who also added HLT54115 Diploma of Nursing had another set of hoops to jump through in order to have this qualification approved on their CRICOS register. This time, the additional requirements come from the *Education Services for Overseas Students (ESOS) Act 2000* as demonstrated in the following discussion.

The CRICOS Register is underpinned by the ESOS Act (s 14A) and as the regulator for the VET sector, ASQA is for the purposes of the ESOS Act, known as the ESOS Agency / Regulator.

LEGAL DECISION-MAKING UNDER THE NATIONAL VOCATIONAL EDUCATION AND TRAINING REGULATOR ACT 2011 (CTH): AN INVESTIGATION INTO ACCESS TO MERITS REVIEW

6C Meaning of *ESOS agency*

(1) Subject to subsections (3) and (4), the following table sets out the ***ESOS agency*** for a provider or registered provider:

ESOS agency		
Item	**To the extent that a provider or registered provider is:**	**the *ESOS agency* for the provider or registered provider is:**
1	a registered higher education provider	TEQSA
2	a registered VET provider	the National VET Regulator
3	an approved school provider	the Secretary
4	a person or entity that provides an ELICOS or a Foundation Program	the entity determined under subsection (2)
5	a provider or registered provider that is not covered by another item of this table	the entity determined under subsection (2)

https://www.legislation.gov.au/Details/C2018C00210

The ESOS Act also provides the basis for the legislated National Code (s 33) and importantly, s 38 refers to what it must contain:

LEGAL DECISION-MAKING UNDER THE NATIONAL VOCATIONAL EDUCATION AND TRAINING REGULATOR ACT 2011 (CTH): AN INVESTIGATION INTO ACCESS TO MERITS REVIEW

38 Contents of the national code

The national code must contain some or all of the following:

(b) standards and procedures required of registered providers in providing courses to overseas students;

(d) standards required of registered providers in connection with their dealings with their agents;

(e) standards required of a registered provider of a course in connection with the provider's dealings with other providers of the course;

(g) standards and procedures required of registered providers in making agreements with overseas students or intending overseas students;

(h) standards required of the content of such agreements;

(i) any other matters that are necessary or convenient to give effect to the purpose of the national code.

https://www.legislation.gov.au/Details/C2018C00210

The National Code, at the time of registering HLT54115 Diploma of Nursing by AIBT has now been superseded by National Code 2018. However, it included requirements similar to those below from National Code 2018:

LEGAL DECISION-MAKING UNDER THE NATIONAL VOCATIONAL EDUCATION AND TRAINING REGULATOR ACT 2011 (CTH): AN INVESTIGATION INTO ACCESS TO MERITS REVIEW

Standard 11

Additional registration requirements

11.1   In applying to register a full-time course at a location, a provider must seek approval from the ESOS agency, including through the relevant designated State authority if the provider is a school, for the following:

11.1.1   the course duration, including holiday breaks

11.1.2   modes of study, including online, distance or work-based training

11.1.3   number of overseas students enrolled at the provider, within the limit or maximum number approved by the ESOS agency for each location

11.1.4   arrangements with other education providers, including partners, in delivering a course or courses to overseas students.

11.2   In seeking approval under 11.1, the provider must demonstrate any matters requested by the ESOS agency, including through the designated State authority if the provider is a school, which may include but are not limited to the following:

11.2.1   the expected duration of the course does not exceed the time required to complete the course on the basis of full-time study – for VET courses, this is a minimum of 20 scheduled course contact hours per week unless specified by an accrediting authority

11.2.2   the expected duration of the course includes any holiday periods or any work-based training

11.2.3   any work-based training to be undertaken as part of the course is necessary for the student to gain the qualification and there are appropriate arrangements for the supervision and assessment of students

11.2.4   the course is not to be delivered entirely by online or distance learning

11.2.5   the provider and any partner they engage to deliver a course or courses to overseas students has adequate staff and education resources, including facilities, equipment, learning and library resources and premises as are needed to deliver the course to the overseas students enrolled with the provider

11.2.6   the maximum number of overseas students proposed by the provider for the location reflects the appropriateness of the staff, resources and facilities for the delivery of the course.

11.3   The registered provider must submit to its ESOS agency for approval, including through the relevant designated State authority if the provider is a school, information on any proposed changes to the provider's registration for a course as outlined in standard 11.1 at least 30 days prior to the time at which those changes are proposed to take effect.

11.4   Registered providers who are self-accrediting must undertake an independent external audit during their period of CRICOS registration, within 18 months prior to renewal of that registration to inform the re-registration of the provider.

LEGAL DECISION-MAKING UNDER THE NATIONAL VOCATIONAL EDUCATION AND TRAINING REGULATOR ACT 2011 (CTH): AN INVESTIGATION INTO ACCESS TO MERITS REVIEW

https://www.legislation.gov.au/Details/F2017L01182/

Html/Text#_Toc487026963

So what is abundantly clear from this is that:

- Not only was AIBT required to demonstrate to the National VET Regulator that they satisfied their legislated registration requirements once for the addition of the course (HLT54115 Diploma of Nursing) to their underpinning scope of registration. But,

- They were also required to do so on a second occasion under completely different legislation by the very same regulator (albeit, this *'audit'* may have occurred concurrently).

As ASQA so clearly states on its website:

LEGAL DECISION-MAKING UNDER THE NATIONAL VOCATIONAL EDUCATION AND TRAINING REGULATOR ACT 2011 (CTH): AN INVESTIGATION INTO ACCESS TO MERITS REVIEW

"Across many industries, Australian Government and state and territory government authorities require a person to possess certain vocational education and training (VET) credentials before that person can be permitted to operate in a particular occupation or vocation. Sometimes a certain VET credential is a prerequisite to gaining an industry operator's licence. In other cases a certain VET credential itself is sufficient industry recognition."

https://www.asqa.gov.au/vet-registration/understand-requirements-registration/other-licensing-and-registration-requirements

As is also stated on the same webpage:

LEGAL DECISION-MAKING UNDER THE NATIONAL VOCATIONAL EDUCATION AND TRAINING REGULATOR ACT 2011 (CTH): AN INVESTIGATION INTO ACCESS TO MERITS REVIEW

"The nominated industry authority may have an arrangement in place with ASQA whereby an application from an RTO (or organisation seeking registration as an RTO) for specified qualifications or units of competency requires evidence of the industry authority's endorsement or support for registration before it can be considered.

These applications will require evidence of pre-application approval from the nominated industry authority by way of supporting documentation. This evidence must be attached at the time of lodgement of application. If evidence is not attached, the application will be considered incomplete."

LEGAL DECISION-MAKING UNDER THE NATIONAL VOCATIONAL EDUCATION AND TRAINING REGULATOR ACT 2011 (CTH): AN INVESTIGATION INTO ACCESS TO MERITS REVIEW

https://www.asqa.gov.au/vet-

registration/understand-requirements-

registration/other-licensing-and-registration-

requirements

As we saw earlier, and repeated for absolute clarity, the ANMAC is listed for both the NVR Act and ESOS Act for HLT54115 Diploma of Nursing:

LEGAL DECISION-MAKING UNDER THE NATIONAL VOCATIONAL EDUCATION AND TRAINING REGULATOR ACT 2011 (CTH): AN INVESTIGATION INTO ACCESS TO MERITS REVIEW

Nominated industry authority arrangements

The following industry sectors are listed as guidance only. Evidence of approval from the relevant government agency/industry body will be required with a registration application.

Industry area	Training product	Application type	Industry authority	Application requirements
Health	HLT54115 Diploma of Nursing	NVR Act*: • Initial registration • Renewal of registration • Addition to scope ESOS Act**: • Initial registration • Renewal of registration • Addition of course	Australian Nursing and Midwifery Accreditation Council (ANMAC)	An application for registration for HLT54115 will only be considered complete if supported by evidence confirming that the applicant organisation has ANMAC accreditation. See the ANMAC website's section on program accreditation. If approved, the organisation must maintain ANMAC accreditation for its entire period of registration for HLT54115.

https://www.asqa.gov.au/vet-registration/understand-requirements-registration/other-licensing-and-registration-requirements

LEGAL DECISION-MAKING UNDER THE NATIONAL VOCATIONAL EDUCATION AND TRAINING REGULATOR ACT 2011 (CTH): AN INVESTIGATION INTO ACCESS TO MERITS REVIEW

Given all of the above, it is absolutely shameful that the National VET Regulator now stands loudly pointing the finger publicly shaming AIBT for a situation that it contributed to! See below ASQA's response to the current issue:

LEGAL DECISION-MAKING UNDER THE NATIONAL VOCATIONAL EDUCATION AND TRAINING REGULATOR ACT 2011 (CTH): AN INVESTIGATION INTO ACCESS TO MERITS REVIEW

The Australian Skills Quality Authority says Brighton Pacific, which trades under the name Australian Institute of Business and Technology, failed to show its marketing was accurate, couldn't demonstrate it met the requirements of its courses, didn't have sufficient staff and had not implemented an assessment system.

ASQA chief commissioner Mark Paterson said it had identified shortcomings in October and a recent review showed the company had not taken remedial action.

The ASQA says it identified shortcomings in October and a recent review showed the company had not taken remedial action. **Wayne Taylor**

"Australia's international student market is large and important and we want to maintain the generally high quality. We look at any providers we think reflect elements of risk. We are not sitting on our hands. If we see a risk we act on it.

"We give warnings that we will target particular areas. In 2017, we said we were targeting international education providers. We've gradually been working through them."

LEGAL DECISION-MAKING UNDER THE NATIONAL VOCATIONAL EDUCATION AND TRAINING REGULATOR ACT 2011 (CTH): AN INVESTIGATION INTO ACCESS TO MERITS REVIEW

Robert Bolton, 20 February 2019, Australian Financial Review
https://www.afr.com/news/policy/education/training-organisation-brighton-pacific-has-registration-cancelled-20190220-h1bi50

One has to question how it even got to the point that AIBT were able to allegedly enrol 2000 international students without ANMAC approval, or without meeting the requirements of the Standards for RTOs and the National Code as explicitly described in this article. If ASQA has approved the course to be on AIBT's scope of registration, it is because:

1. ASQA found that it did have ANMAC approval (*or ASQA breached its own Standards*); and

2. ASQA also found it compliant against Clause 1.8 of the Standards for RTOs 2015 at an absolute minimum (*or ASQA breached its own Standards*); and

176

LEGAL DECISION-MAKING UNDER THE
NATIONAL VOCATIONAL EDUCATION AND
TRAINING REGULATOR ACT 2011 (CTH): AN
INVESTIGATION INTO ACCESS TO MERITS
REVIEW

3. ASQA also found that AIBT satisfied Standard 11 of the National Code (although at the time, it would have been National Code 2007, Part D, Standard 14) *or ASQA breached its own Standards*.

It is the writer's opinion that it is inappropriate for the Chief Commissioner to be calling out AIBT in this manner (*even if it is found to have done the wrong thing*). The Chief Commissioner should also be looking internally as a matter of absolute priority and urgency at the manner in which its auditors conduct their investigations into whether or not providers are meeting these additional accreditation/licensing/registration requirements.

If the National VET Regulator was truly meeting its legislative functions in relation to this issue, it would be engaging with other regulators and using their technical expertise to ensure that the National VET Regulator can

LEGAL DECISION-MAKING UNDER THE NATIONAL VOCATIONAL EDUCATION AND TRAINING REGULATOR ACT 2011 (CTH): AN INVESTIGATION INTO ACCESS TO MERITS REVIEW

perform its duties adequately under its legislative obligations. To not do so, and then point the finger shows a complete disregard for the legislative provisions that underpin the very existence of the National VET Regulator and compromise the integrity of the Australian VET sector more than the behaviour of AIBT allegedly can through this issue because it is surely not restricted to this sole instance.

Just as the regulator finds systematic breaches of compliance obligations amongst the providers it regulates, in my own practice I have witnessed and experienced the systematic failure by the National VET Regulator to engage with other regulators to perform their legislative duty; this problem is much bigger than AIBT. The public (*and the judiciary*) are just not being made aware of how big an issue this really is.

LEGAL DECISION-MAKING UNDER THE NATIONAL VOCATIONAL EDUCATION AND TRAINING REGULATOR ACT 2011 (CTH): AN INVESTIGATION INTO ACCESS TO MERITS REVIEW

While I do not condone what AIBT has allegedly done, I believe that it is merely a scapegoat for a system that has serious, complex and systematic deficiencies…and like many things, it all begins at the top.

LEGAL DECISION-MAKING UNDER THE NATIONAL VOCATIONAL EDUCATION AND TRAINING REGULATOR ACT 2011 (CTH): AN INVESTIGATION INTO ACCESS TO MERITS REVIEW

Business Institute of Australia Pty Ltd (BIA)

Neither the author or RTO Doctor have any current association with BIA, and the author provides comment on the issues based solely on publicly available information, namely, the Decision and Reasons for Decision available on the AustLii database at the following link http://www.austlii.edu.au/cgi-bin/viewdoc/au/cases/cth/AATA/2019/699.html

The author has no knowledge of the audit or operational processes that led to this situation.

LEGAL DECISION-MAKING UNDER THE NATIONAL VOCATIONAL EDUCATION AND TRAINING REGULATOR ACT 2011 (CTH): AN INVESTIGATION INTO ACCESS TO MERITS REVIEW

The case of BIA is actually in relation to three (3) RTO registrations:

- Business Institute of Australia (RTOID: 91019);

- Wells International College (RTOID: 90501); and

- Warwick Institute of Australia (RTOID: 91270).

All RTOs applied collectively to the Tribunal.

Context

At the time of the application to the Tribunal, BIA had been an RTO since 2004 (15 years), had invested expenses of approximately $A850K in a fit out of premises including computers and furniture. It had 574 overseas students enrolled.

LEGAL DECISION-MAKING UNDER THE
NATIONAL VOCATIONAL EDUCATION AND
TRAINING REGULATOR ACT 2011 (CTH): AN
INVESTIGATION INTO ACCESS TO MERITS
REVIEW

WIA had been an RTO since 2006 (13 years) and had invested approximately $A500K into the fit out of its premises in 2009 and a further $A350K in 2017 fitting out a new campus in Brisbane. It had 505 overseas students enrolled.

A similar amount was invested by WIC which had been an RTO since 1998 (19 years). It had 698 overseas students enrolled.

The RTOs had never had any conditions placed on their registrations in their entire registration periods that required them to monitor attendance. At paragraph 39 of the reasons for the Decision, we see that the RTOs all were operating on a course progress policy provision and not attendance as is permitted under Clauses 8.1 and 8.9 of the National Code 2018. In fact, every overseas student who was enrolled in these RTOs entered a contract with the relevant RTO that they agreed to a

182
LEGAL DECISION-MAKING UNDER THE
NATIONAL VOCATIONAL EDUCATION AND
TRAINING REGULATOR ACT 2011 (CTH): AN
INVESTIGATION INTO ACCESS TO MERITS
REVIEW

course progress policy, not a course attendance policy. Clause 8.10 of the National Code only applies where a condition has been imposed by the ESOS Agency (in this case, ASQA).

An important outcome of this matter was that ASQA was ordered to:

> '*take all measures reasonably available to it to remove from any website under its control any publication of the Decision and all the conditions imposed by the Decision*'

And within 72 hours and were to:

> '*refrain from publishing the Decision and all the conditions imposed by it until further order of the Tribunal*'.

LEGAL DECISION-MAKING UNDER THE NATIONAL VOCATIONAL EDUCATION AND TRAINING REGULATOR ACT 2011 (CTH): AN INVESTIGATION INTO ACCESS TO MERITS REVIEW

This important decision relates back to earlier content in the book regarding reputational damage.

This case has been selected for commentary based on ASQA's recent media release referred to earlier when it responded to The Honourable Ian Callinan's findings in the AAT Review. ASQA's representative denied making comments to the respected former High Court of Australia judge Ian Callinan, the author behind the Review.

ASQA's comments were:

> "She told me that delays in making decisions had repercussions beyond the AAT.
> "ASQA was aware that organised crime was sometimes, perhaps even regularly, benefiting from counterfeit vocational training programs and colleges," Mr Callinan said in his report.

LEGAL DECISION-MAKING UNDER THE NATIONAL VOCATIONAL EDUCATION AND TRAINING REGULATOR ACT 2011 (CTH): AN INVESTIGATION INTO ACCESS TO MERITS REVIEW

As per Tim Dodd in The Australian newspaper on 25 July 2019:

> In his review, Mr Callinan also said that in his meeting with ASQA's acting head, she had cited so-called "ghost colleges" for international students as an -example of organised crime's involvement in the vocational training industry.

> He said she had discussed with him the fact that these colleges were "little more than addresses operated by people who provided no real training or tuition".

> "Their 'students' were not bona fide students. Often the so-called provider would find a job for the foreign entrant, charging commissions to both the employer and the so-called 'student employee',

LEGAL DECISION-MAKING UNDER THE NATIONAL VOCATIONAL EDUCATION AND TRAINING REGULATOR ACT 2011 (CTH): AN INVESTIGATION INTO ACCESS TO MERITS REVIEW

and arrange, again at cost, the transmission of funds to the 'student's' home country," Mr Callinan wrote in his review.

The Decision and Reasons for Decision in the BIA case, as referred to earlier in this book, clearly demonstrate that the actions of ASQA in the matter of BIA 100% support Callinan's findings and the comments that he claimed were made by ASQA. The behaviour described in the Reasons for Decision handed down by the Tribunal Member further demonstrate the cultural belief that ASQA has as an organisation in relation to 'ghost colleges'.

At paragraphs 5 and 6 of the Reasons for the Decision in BIA, we see a common approach used by ASQA when conducting investigations.

LEGAL DECISION-MAKING UNDER THE NATIONAL VOCATIONAL EDUCATION AND TRAINING REGULATOR ACT 2011 (CTH): AN INVESTIGATION INTO ACCESS TO MERITS REVIEW

The lack of announcement or provision of notice, often announcing that they wish to enter or if their entrance is denied, the RTO will be in breach of Standard 8 of the *Standards for Registered Training Organisations 2015*. They make it very clear that if access is denied, officers will obtain a warrant for entry. Their behaviour is aggressive, intimidatory and intends to cause fear. The use of cameras and unexpected interviewing of staff and students, demands for documentation, removal of evidence all demonstrate behaviour that can only be described as designed to induce fear and intimidate providers.

I personally have been in attendance in such situations (*although not in this matter*) and the ASQA officers involved did come across in this manner causing immense fear to providers.

LEGAL DECISION-MAKING UNDER THE NATIONAL VOCATIONAL EDUCATION AND TRAINING REGULATOR ACT 2011 (CTH): AN INVESTIGATION INTO ACCESS TO MERITS REVIEW

The ASQA officers in attendance, embarrassingly for the National VET Regulator, announced themselves under the wrong section of the *National Vocational Education and Training Regulator Act 2011* (Cth) ("NVR Act"), one of the officers was not even eligible at the time to announce himself under that section of the Act because as a Contractor, the legislative provision did not apply to him. He suddenly returned a few hours later as an employee of ASQA instead with a comment that his paperwork had been in the process of being finalised and was now appropriate. They intimidated staff, students and passers-by and conducted themselves like Police Officers on a witch-hunt. As such, the matter of BIA has been selected on the basis described.

At paragraph 5 of the Reasons for the Decision, we see the following:

LEGAL DECISION-MAKING UNDER THE NATIONAL VOCATIONAL EDUCATION AND TRAINING REGULATOR ACT 2011 (CTH): AN INVESTIGATION INTO ACCESS TO MERITS REVIEW

- At approximately 10.30am…Without prior notice…to check the attendance at each class…A camera was used to film the activities.
- On the same day at 2.30pm again without prior notice, the same officers entered BIA's premises…they walked around…to check the attendance of classes and again used a camera to film…A copy of the student attendance record…was photocopied.

At paragraphs 13, 15 and 16, we see another demonstration of how ASQA's behaviour is consistent with an organisational culture that believes that there are 'ghost colleges':

- ASQA further alleged that…whereas 46 students were said to be enrolled…only one student

LEGAL DECISION-MAKING UNDER THE NATIONAL VOCATIONAL EDUCATION AND TRAINING REGULATOR ACT 2011 (CTH): AN INVESTIGATION INTO ACCESS TO MERITS REVIEW

attended...another course...of 33 enrolled, there was no attendance; in Room 3, 35 students were meant to be in attendance but only 2 were in attendance...in Room 4, 10 students were enrolled but...no students were present in the room.

- The intention letter also stated that ASQA was concerned that the colleges were failing to ensure students met minimum attendance requirements.
- The intention letter stated that ASQA considered that the provider's attendance records required by Standard 8 of the National Code showed significant levels of non-attendance, it could indicate that the provider was not complying with the obligations under clause 1.1 and clause 1.2 of the Standards for RTOs and clause 11.2.1 of the National Code...

LEGAL DECISION-MAKING UNDER THE NATIONAL VOCATIONAL EDUCATION AND TRAINING REGULATOR ACT 2011 (CTH): AN INVESTIGATION INTO ACCESS TO MERITS REVIEW

There are a number of concerns regarding this intention letter which the Tribunal Member, in my opinion, made the correct and preferable decision at the stay hearing. They are addressed next.

LEGAL DECISION-MAKING UNDER THE NATIONAL VOCATIONAL EDUCATION AND TRAINING REGULATOR ACT 2011 (CTH): AN INVESTIGATION INTO ACCESS TO MERITS REVIEW

Student Enrolment Contracts and Consumer Law

The enrolment of any student in a VET course with an RTO is a contract. This is recognised by Standards 3 and 5 of the Standards for RTOs that are entirely relevant to and aligned with the consumer protection provisions of Australian Consumer Law.

Clause 2.1.8 of the National Code 2018 provides the basis for a cancellation of enrolment by the student or the provider which then links to Standard 3 as the student's enrolment is subsequently formalised into a contract on the recruitment information referred to below:

> 2.1.8 the **grounds on which the overseas student's enrolment may be** deferred, suspended **or cancelled**

LEGAL DECISION-MAKING UNDER THE NATIONAL VOCATIONAL EDUCATION AND TRAINING REGULATOR ACT 2011 (CTH): AN INVESTIGATION INTO ACCESS TO MERITS REVIEW

Clause 3.4.5 states:

> a statement that "**This written agreement**, and the right to make complaints and seek appeals of decisions and action under various processes, **does not affect the rights of the student to take action under the** *Australian Consumer Law* **if** the *Australian Consumer Law* **applies**".

For example, clause 5.3(b) which states:

> 5.3 Where the RTO collects fees from the individual learner, either directly or through a third party, **the RTO provides or directs the learner to information prior to enrolment** or the commencement of training and assessment, whichever comes first, specifying:

LEGAL DECISION-MAKING UNDER THE NATIONAL VOCATIONAL EDUCATION AND TRAINING REGULATOR ACT 2011 (CTH): AN INVESTIGATION INTO ACCESS TO MERITS REVIEW

(b) **the learner's rights as a consumer**, including but not limited to any statutory cooling-off period, if one applies;

In respect of the RTOs concerned in this matter, their concerns were at all times that their students had been contracted to the RTOs under the condition that their attendance would be monitored in accordance with the course progress requirements of the National Code 2018 and not monitoring course attendance.

If the RTOs had suddenly complied with ASQA's request, they would have potentially been in breach of contract with each of their overseas students. In other words, they might have been in breach of contract with:

- 574 students at BIA;
- 505 overseas students at WIA; and
- 698 overseas students at WIC.

LEGAL DECISION-MAKING UNDER THE NATIONAL VOCATIONAL EDUCATION AND TRAINING REGULATOR ACT 2011 (CTH): AN INVESTIGATION INTO ACCESS TO MERITS REVIEW

Under Australian Consumer Law, if an RTO fails to meet the consumer guarantee in the contract, the consumer is entitled to recover damages, and in some circumstances, additional damages. Therefore, if the RTO had to cancel its current contract because one of the key conditions of delivery of that service is being changed, every student was within their rights to seek a refund and to terminate their contract with the respective RTO. This could have also potentially activated the Tuition Protection Service unnecessarily and caused unnecessary expense to the Australian taxpayer to manage the transfer or refund of approximately 1327 overseas students.

The reason, just to be explicit:

ASQA was mandating a requirement of attendance on their enrolment in their respective courses that the student did not agree to in their contracts with their

LEGAL DECISION-MAKING UNDER THE NATIONAL VOCATIONAL EDUCATION AND TRAINING REGULATOR ACT 2011 (CTH): AN INVESTIGATION INTO ACCESS TO MERITS REVIEW

respective RTO. The respective RTOs were, like thousands of other CRICOS registered RTOs monitoring course progress in accordance with Clause 8.9 and were not, by law required to implement a course attendance monitoring policy.

LEGAL DECISION-MAKING UNDER THE NATIONAL VOCATIONAL EDUCATION AND TRAINING REGULATOR ACT 2011 (CTH): AN INVESTIGATION INTO ACCESS TO MERITS REVIEW

Course Progress Monitoring and Attendance Requirements under the National Code 2018

Clause 5 of the National Code 2018 is linked to the previous consumer protection provisions and states:

> 8.5　　　The
>
> registered provider **must clearly outline　and inform the　　overseas student before they commence the course**
>
> of the requirements to achieve satisfactory course progress **and, where applicable,** attendance in each study period.

Clauses 8.9 and 8.10 of the National Code 2018 are reproduced below to demonstrate these points. Relevant sections are highlighted.

LEGAL DECISION-MAKING UNDER THE NATIONAL VOCATIONAL EDUCATION AND TRAINING REGULATOR ACT 2011 (CTH): AN INVESTIGATION INTO ACCESS TO MERITS REVIEW

Course progress monitoring:

Vocational education and training (VET): course progress and attendance requirements

8.9   The registered provider of a VET course as defined in the NVETR Act must have and implement a documented policy and process for assessing course progress that includes:

8.9.1   requirements for achieving satis factory course progress, includi ng policies that promote and uphold the academic integrity o f the registered course and meet the training package or accredited course requirements where appl icable, and processes to address misconduct and allegati ons of misconduct

198

LEGAL DECISION-MAKING UNDER THE
NATIONAL VOCATIONAL EDUCATION AND
TRAINING REGULATOR ACT 2011 (CTH): AN
INVESTIGATION INTO ACCESS TO MERITS
REVIEW

8.9.2	processes for recording and assessing course progress requirements
8.9.3	processes to identify overseas students at risk of unsatisfactory course progress
8.9.4	details of the registered provider's intervention strategy to assist overseas students at risk of not meeting course progress requirements in sufficient time for those overseas students to achieve satisfactory course progress
8.9.5	processes for determining the point at which the overseas student has failed to meet satisfactory course progress.

And for attendance monitoring:

LEGAL DECISION-MAKING UNDER THE NATIONAL VOCATIONAL EDUCATION AND TRAINING REGULATOR ACT 2011 (CTH): AN INVESTIGATION INTO ACCESS TO MERITS REVIEW

8.10   The registered provider must have and implement a documented policy and process for monitoring the attendance of overseas students **if the requirement to implement and maintain minimum attendance requirements for overseas students is set as a condition of the provider's registration by an ESOS agency**.

Clause 6.1 provides for information that is usually presented to students at their compulsory orientation session upon commencement at their RTO and states:

LEGAL DECISION-MAKING UNDER THE NATIONAL VOCATIONAL EDUCATION AND TRAINING REGULATOR ACT 2011 (CTH): AN INVESTIGATION INTO ACCESS TO MERITS REVIEW

6.1.7   requirements for course attendance an d progress, **as appropriate**

As can be seen through these excerpts of legislation, effectively what ASQA was demanding that the RTOs do would have been a contravention of the National Code 2018 and breached their obligations under Australian Consumer Law. And one has to ask on what basis? While there may not have been students in attendance in those classrooms on those days, there was no mandatory requirement for any of them to be there in the first place because at all times, no student was attending under a monitoring course progress policy. When the CEO provided evidence to the Tribunal that students would leave and go to another RTO who operated on a course progress policy, this is the reason why. Students would be seriously disadvantaged and be forced into a position that they never agreed to when enrolling.

The issue of monitoring course progress and monitoring course attendance has long been an issue of concern to the National VET Regulator. This is further compounded by the fact that monitoring course progress and attendance are both linked to Australia's migration program and international student visa conditions. Indeed, the condition 8202 that is referred to in this matter is referred to below:

- remain enrolled in a registered course;
- maintain enrolment in a registered course that is the same **Australian Qualifications Framework (AQF)** level or higher for which the visa was granted;

- maintain satisfactory attendance and course progress for each study period as required by the education provider.

What can be seen is a monitoring policy that has been delegated from the Department of Home Affairs (Immigration) to the Department of Education. RTOs are then obliged to report their findings via a shared database between the Department of Home Affairs, the Department of Education and the RTO. Sadly, the 2 Commonwealth departments do not appear to sufficiently talk to each other to:

- enable meaningful legislation to be drafted to ensure that the monitoring is done legally, effectively, in accordance with Australian Consumer Law provisions so that no international student is negatively impacted; or

LEGAL DECISION-MAKING UNDER THE NATIONAL VOCATIONAL EDUCATION AND TRAINING REGULATOR ACT 2011 (CTH): AN INVESTIGATION INTO ACCESS TO MERITS REVIEW

- ensure that no RTO is forced into a position that it should never have been placed because the delegated regulator (ASQA) potentially did not understand the requirement, its operation and the impact of decisions made on the basis of that misinterpretation.

In summary, the Tribunal Member, at paragraph 57 rightly stated:

> The Code is a statutory instrument. It is difficult, at this stage, to see how the respondent can impose a condition which might be inconsistent with the provisions of a statutory instrument...It would place the applicants in an invidious position if they committed a breach of the conditions when the condition was founded upon an invalid premise or was interpreted incorrectly by ASQA.

LEGAL DECISION-MAKING UNDER THE NATIONAL VOCATIONAL EDUCATION AND TRAINING REGULATOR ACT 2011 (CTH): AN INVESTIGATION INTO ACCESS TO MERITS REVIEW

At paragraph 61, the Tribunal Member correctly found that:

> The public interest requires that the regulation of providers be strictly observed. However, it must be observed in accordance with the statutory requirements, including the requirements of the Code.

This is exactly what this research and this book has been about. The writer, and RTO Doctor agree that there is a need for regulation, this is not disputed. However, that regulation must be undertaken in accordance with legislative provisions, in accordance with natural justice and following procedural fairness. It must also follow that regulation is conducted in a way that aligns with the Commonwealth Government's Deregulation Agenda

LEGAL DECISION-MAKING UNDER THE NATIONAL VOCATIONAL EDUCATION AND TRAINING REGULATOR ACT 2011 (CTH): AN INVESTIGATION INTO ACCESS TO MERITS REVIEW

and that it acts in accordance with the framework that that agenda is founded upon, a commitment to best practice regulation to improve regulatory quality.

LEGAL DECISION-MAKING UNDER THE NATIONAL VOCATIONAL EDUCATION AND TRAINING REGULATOR ACT 2011 (CTH): AN INVESTIGATION INTO ACCESS TO MERITS REVIEW

Bibliography

A *Articles/Books/Reports*

Administrative Review Committee, Administrative Review Committee Report, Parl Paper No 144 (1971)

Administrative Review Council, *Better Decisions: Review Of The Commonwealth Merits Review Tribunals* (Report to the Minister for Justice No 39, 1995)

Australian Skills Quality Authority, *ASQA Annual Report 2017-2018*

Chris Conybeare, 'The Structure of the Commonwealth Merits Review Tribunal System' (1995) 12 *AIAL Forum No 7* 28

Dawn Watkins and Mandy Burton (ed), *Research Methods in Law, Second Edition* (Routledge, 2018)

LEGAL DECISION-MAKING UNDER THE NATIONAL VOCATIONAL EDUCATION AND TRAINING REGULATOR ACT 2011 (CTH): AN INVESTIGATION INTO ACCESS TO MERITS REVIEW

Diana Young and Nadja Zimmerman, 'Procedural Fairness in Administrative Decision-Making' (2016) 18 *Precedent, Sydney NSW* 136

Judith Bannister and Anna Olijnyk, *Government Accountability - Australian Administrative Law, Sources and Materials,* (Cambridge University Press NS, 2018)

Judith Bannister, Anna Olijnyk and Stephen McDonald, *Government Accountability - Australian Administrative Law,* (Cambridge University Press NS, 2nd Edition, 2018)

Katherine Hooper, 'Model Litigants, Migration, Merits Review And … Mediation?' (2013) 157 *University of Queensland Law Journal* 28

Kay Bowman and Suzy McKenna, *The Development of Australia's National Training System: A Dynamic Tension Between Consistency and Flexibility* (NCVER, 2016)

LexisNexis Concise Australian Legal Dictionary (5th ed, 2015)

LEGAL DECISION-MAKING UNDER THE NATIONAL VOCATIONAL EDUCATION AND TRAINING REGULATOR ACT 2011 (CTH): AN INVESTIGATION INTO ACCESS TO MERITS REVIEW

Michael D. Tovey and Diane R. Lawlor, *Training in Australia, Third Edition* (Pearson Education Australia, 2008)

Prof. Tushar Kanti Saha, *Textbook on Legal Methods, Legal Systems & Research* (Universal Law Publishing, 2nd ed, 2015)

Robert Todd AM, 'The Structure of the Commonwealth Merits Review Tribunal System' (1995) 12 *AIAL Forum No 7* 33

Robin Creyke et al, *Laying Down The Law* (LexisNexis Butterworths, 10th ed, 2018)

Robin Todd and Muriel Dunbar, UNESCO, 'Taking A Whole of Government Approach to Skills Development' (2018)

Roger Fernandez et al, *Australian Migration Legislation Collection June 2018* (LexisNexis Butterworths, 2018)

Sarah Withnall Howe and Michelle Evans, *Administrative Law*, (LexisNexis Butterworths, 2nd ed, 2015)

LEGAL DECISION-MAKING UNDER THE NATIONAL VOCATIONAL EDUCATION AND TRAINING REGULATOR ACT 2011 (CTH): AN INVESTIGATION INTO ACCESS TO MERITS REVIEW

Terry Hutchinson, *Researching and Writing in Law* (Thomson Reuters Professional, 4th ed, 2018)

The Hon Ian Callinan AC, *Review: Section 4 of the Tribunals Amalgamation Act 2015 (Cth) Report*, (July 2019)

Valerie Braithwaite, *All Eyes on Quality: Review of the National Vocational Education and Training Regulator Act 2011 Report* (January 2018)

W. Lawrence Neuman, *Social Research Methods: Qualitative and Quantitative Approaches, Third Edition* (Allynn and Bacon, 1997)

LEGAL DECISION-MAKING UNDER THE NATIONAL VOCATIONAL EDUCATION AND TRAINING REGULATOR ACT 2011 (CTH): AN INVESTIGATION INTO ACCESS TO MERITS REVIEW

B *Cases*

Anthony Scott v Australian Securities and Investment Commission (2009) 51 AAR 114

Australian Academy of Management & Science Pty Ltd v Australian Skills Quality Authority [2013] AATA 530 (30 July 2013)

Australian Broadcasting Tribunal v Bond [1990] HCA 33

Australian Business Skills Pty Ltd v Australian Skills Quality Authority [2012] NSWADT 133 (5 July 2012)

Australian Business Skills Pty Ltd v Australian Skills Quality Authority [2013] NSWADTAP 9 (19 February 2013)

Australian Careers Institute Pty Ltd and Australian Skills Quality Authority [2016] AATA 730 (21 September 2016)

Australian Competition and Consumer Commission v Get Qualified Australia Pty Ltd [2016] FCA 976 (18 August 2016)

LEGAL DECISION-MAKING UNDER THE NATIONAL VOCATIONAL EDUCATION AND TRAINING REGULATOR ACT 2011 (CTH): AN INVESTIGATION INTO ACCESS TO MERITS REVIEW

Australian Competition and Consumer Commission v Unique International College Pty Ltd [2017] FCA 727 (30 June 2017)

Australian Institute of Professional Education Pty Limited v Australian Skills Quality Authority [2016] FCA 814 (13 July 2016)

Australian Institute of Technical Training Pty Ltd v Australian Skills Quality Authority [2018] AATA 1281 (11 May 2018)

Sher-E-Punjab Pty Ltd v Australian Skills Quality Authority [2018] AATA 46 (15 January 2018)

Australian Institute of Trades Pty Ltd as trustee for the Institute of Hotel Management Australia v Australian Skills Quality Authority [2017] AATA 2912 (1 August 2017)

Australian International College Pty Ltd v Australian Skills Quality Authority [2018] FCA 2097

Australian Trade Training and Assessment Pty Ltd (ATTA) v Australian Skills Quality Authority [2019] AATA 231 (25 January 2019)

LEGAL DECISION-MAKING UNDER THE NATIONAL VOCATIONAL EDUCATION AND TRAINING REGULATOR ACT 2011 (CTH): AN INVESTIGATION INTO ACCESS TO MERITS REVIEW

Australian Vocational Driving Institute Pty Ltd and Australian Skills Quality Authority [2014] AATA 892 (20 November 2014)

Australian Vocational Driving Institute Pty Ltd and Australian Skills Quality Authority [2014] AATA 889 (1 December 2014)

Australian Vocational Learning Centre Pty Ltd v Australian Skills Quality Authority [2018] AATA 4725 (21 December 2018)

Austwide Institute of Training Pty Ltd v Australian Skills Quality Authority [2014] FCA 768 (30 July 2014)

Avetmiss Easy Pty Ltd and Australian Skills Quality Authority [2013] AATA 732 (17 September 2013)

Avetmiss Easy Pty Ltd and Australian Skills Quality Authority [2014] FCA 46 (7 February 2014)

Avetmiss Easy Pty Ltd and Australian Skills Quality Authority [2014] AATA 99 (24 February 2014)

LEGAL DECISION-MAKING UNDER THE NATIONAL VOCATIONAL EDUCATION AND TRAINING REGULATOR ACT 2011 (CTH): AN INVESTIGATION INTO ACCESS TO MERITS REVIEW

Avetmiss Easy Pty Ltd and Australian Skills Quality Authority [2014] FCA 314 (4 April 2014)

Avetmiss Easy Pty Ltd and Australian Skills Quality Authority [2014] FCA 444 (7 May 2014)

Avetmiss Easy Pty Ltd and Australian Skills Quality Authority [2014] FCA 507 (19 May 2014)

Avetmiss Easy Pty Ltd and Australian Skills Quality Authority [2014] FCA 761 (19 May 2014)

BJSB Pty Ltd (t/a The Imperial College of Australia) v Australian Skills Quality Authority [2019] AATA 1053 (30 May 2019)

Business Institute of Australia Pty Ltd v Australian Skills Quality Authority [2019] AATA 669 (16 April 2019) *Metro College of Technology Pty Ltd and Australian Skills Quality Authority* (Unreported)

C.A.R.E Employment & Training Services Pty Ltd v Australian Skills Quality Authority [2012] FCA 367 (3 April 2012)

LEGAL DECISION-MAKING UNDER THE NATIONAL VOCATIONAL EDUCATION AND TRAINING REGULATOR ACT 2011 (CTH): AN INVESTIGATION INTO ACCESS TO MERITS REVIEW

Cambridge International College (Vic) Pty Ltd v Australian Skills Quality Authority and Anor [2013] AATA 805 (13 November 2013)

Chemcert Training Group v Australian Skills Quality Authority [2019] AATA 313 (4 March 2019)

Claredale Academy Pty Ltd v Australian Skills Quality Authority [2019] AATA 1869 (12 July 2019)

Daily Update Pty Ltd v Australian Skills Quality Authority [2014] AATA 118 (6 March 2014)

Darwin Human Resource and Computer Academy Pty Ltd v Australian Skills Quality Authority [2017] AATA 738 (24 May 2017)

Devkota and Australian Skills Quality Authority [2015] AATA 356 (22 May 2015)

Echelon National Security Agency Pty Ltd v Australian Skills Quality Authority [2013] AATA 602 (27 August 2013)

Echelon National Security Agency Pty Ltd v Australian Skills Quality Authority [2014] AATA 151 (25 February 2014)

LEGAL DECISION-MAKING UNDER THE NATIONAL VOCATIONAL EDUCATION AND TRAINING REGULATOR ACT 2011 (CTH): AN INVESTIGATION INTO ACCESS TO MERITS REVIEW

Echelon National Security Agency Pty Ltd v Australian Skills Quality Authority [2014] AATA 761 (24 July 2014)

Elite Academy Australia Pty Ltd v Australian Skills Quality Authority [2019] AATA 79 (5 February 2019)

G Plus G Global Trading Pty Ltd v Australian Skills Quality Authority [2013] AATA 698 (23 September 2013)

Greenfield Education Pty Ltd v Australian Skills Quality Authority [2018] AATA 4210 (9 November 2018)

Griffith University v Tang (2005) 221 CLR 99

Gurkhas Institute of Technology Pty Ltd trading as Gurkhas Institute of Technology v Australian Skills Quality Authority [2017] AATA 1018 (3 July 2017)

Institute of Training Pty Ltd v Australian Skills Quality Authority [2018] AATA 4127 (5 November 2018)

International School of Professional Skills Pty Ltd v Australian Skills Quality Authority [2012] AATA 287 (16 April 2012)

Ivy Education Group Pty Ltd and Australian Skills Quality Authority [2013] AATA 138 (14 March 2013)

LEGAL DECISION-MAKING UNDER THE NATIONAL VOCATIONAL EDUCATION AND TRAINING REGULATOR ACT 2011 (CTH): AN INVESTIGATION INTO ACCESS TO MERITS REVIEW

Menzies Institute of Technology v Australian Skills Quality Authority [2019] AATA 343 (12 February 2019)

New South Wales Thoroughbred Racing Board v Waterhouse (2003) 56 NSWLR 691, 711

Oztech Trade Training college Pty Ltd v Australian Skills Quality Authority [2018] AATA 3741 (9 October 2018)

Pacific Flight Services Pty Ltd v Australian Skills Quality Authority [2019] AATA 745 (23 April 2019)

Phoenix Institute of Australia Pty Ltd v Commonwealth of Australia [2016] FCA 190 (4 March 2016)

Pow Wow Training Pty Ltd v Australian Skills Quality Authority [2012] FCA1490 (20 November 2012)

Pow Wow Training Pty Ltd v Australian Skills Quality Authority [2012] FCA1245 (7 November 2012)

RAMC Pty Ltd and Australian Skills Quality Authority [2015] AATA 306 (7 May 2015)

Real Training Outcomes v Australian Skills Quality Authority [2018] AATA 4611 (18 December 2018)

LEGAL DECISION-MAKING UNDER THE NATIONAL VOCATIONAL EDUCATION AND TRAINING REGULATOR ACT 2011 (CTH): AN INVESTIGATION INTO ACCESS TO MERITS REVIEW

Security Training and Tactics Pty Ltd v Australian Skills Quality Authority [2012] NSWADT 178 (29 August 2012)

Shvetsova V University of New England [2014] NSWSC 918

Skilled Education Australia Pty Limited v Australian Skills Quality Authority [2019] AATA 317 (4 March 2019)

Snook and Civil Aviation Safety Authority [2008] AATA 861; (2008) 109 ALD 122

Success Fast-Track Pty Ltd v Australian Skills Quality Authority [2012] AATA 531 (10 August 2012)

Sunrise Institute of Australia Pty Ltd v Australian Skills Quality Authority [2018] AATA 3935 (15 October 2018

Sunrise Institute of Australia Pty Ltd v Australian Skills Quality Authority [2019] AATA 1131 (5 June 2019)

Sydney Training Academy Pty Ltd and Australian Skills Quality Authority [2018] AATA 3361 (7 September 2018)

Technical Education Australia Pty Ltd v Australian Skills Quality Authority [2018] AATA 3047 (23 August 2018)

LEGAL DECISION-MAKING UNDER THE NATIONAL VOCATIONAL EDUCATION AND TRAINING REGULATOR ACT 2011 (CTH): AN INVESTIGATION INTO ACCESS TO MERITS REVIEW

Trades College Australia Pty Ltd v Australian Skills Quality Authority [2018] AATA 1703 (12 June 2018)

Unique International College Pty Ltd v Australian Council for Private Education and Training [2016] NSWSC 607 (12 May 2016)

VETiS Consulting Services Pty Ltd v Australian Skills Quality Authority [2019] AATA 341 (7 March 2019)

Walsh v University of Technology, Sydney [2007] FCA 880

Western Institute of Technology Pty Ltd v Australian Skills Quality Authority [2018] AATA 94 (25 January 2018)

LEGAL DECISION-MAKING UNDER THE NATIONAL VOCATIONAL EDUCATION AND TRAINING REGULATOR ACT 2011 (CTH): AN INVESTIGATION INTO ACCESS TO MERITS REVIEW

C Legislation

Administrative Appeals Tribunal Act 1975 (Cth)

Administrative Decisions (Judicial Review) Act 1977 (Cth)

Australian Qualifications Framework (2nd Edition)

Data Collection Requirements 2012 (Cth)

Education Services for Overseas Students 2000 - Foundation Program Standards

Education Services for Overseas Students Act 2000 (Cth)

ELICOS Standards 2018 (Cth)

Financial Viability Risk Assessment Requirements 2011 (Cth)

Fit and Proper Persons Requirements 2011 (Cth)

Legal Services Directions 2017 (Cth)

National Vocational Education and Training Regulator Act 2011 (Cth)

Standards for Registered Training Organisations (RTOs) 2015 (Cth)

Standards for VET Accredited Courses 2012 (Cth);

Standards for VET Regulators 2015 (Cth)

LEGAL DECISION-MAKING UNDER THE NATIONAL VOCATIONAL EDUCATION AND TRAINING REGULATOR ACT 2011 (CTH): AN INVESTIGATION INTO ACCESS TO MERITS REVIEW

The *National Code of Practice for Providers of Education and Training to Overseas Students 2018*

LEGAL DECISION-MAKING UNDER THE NATIONAL VOCATIONAL EDUCATION AND TRAINING REGULATOR ACT 2011 (CTH): AN INVESTIGATION INTO ACCESS TO MERITS REVIEW

D *Other*

Administrative Appeals Tribunal, 'Decision', (Web Page) <https://www.aat.gov.au/steps-in-a-review/other-decisions/decision>

Australian Skills Authority, '*About Australia's VET Sector*', (Web Page) <https://www.asqa.gov.au/about/australias-vet-sector>

Australian Skills Authority, '*Changes to ASQA's Decision-Making Processes*', (Web Page) < https://www.asqa.gov.au/news-publications/media/asqa-announces-further-changes-protect-sectorhttps://www.asqa.gov.au/news-publications/media/asqa-announces-further-changes-protect-sector>

Australian Skills Quality Authority, 'APS6 - Lead Auditor', Federal Government Career (Archived Advertisement, 04 May 2018)

LEGAL DECISION-MAKING UNDER THE NATIONAL VOCATIONAL EDUCATION AND TRAINING REGULATOR ACT 2011 (CTH): AN INVESTIGATION INTO ACCESS TO MERITS REVIEW

<federal.governmentcareer.com.au/jobs/8282-australian-skills-quality-authority-asqa/60615>

Australian Skills Quality Authority, 'ASQA's New Audit Approach Evaluation Report: Key Findings and Recommendations (Evaluation Report, February 2017) <https://www.asqa.gov.au/sites/default/files/asqas_new_audit_approach_evaluation_report_-_key_findings_and_recommendations.pdf?v=1508300289>

Australian Skills Quality Authority, 'ASQA's New Audit Model' (Report) <https://www.asqa.gov.au/sites/default/files/asqas_new_audit_model.pdf?v=1539231343>

Australian Skills Quality Authority, 'Australian Skills Quality Authority's Submission To the Review of the National Vocational Education and Training Regulator Act 2011' (Submission)

LEGAL DECISION-MAKING UNDER THE
NATIONAL VOCATIONAL EDUCATION AND
TRAINING REGULATOR ACT 2011 (CTH): AN
INVESTIGATION INTO ACCESS TO MERITS
REVIEW

<https://www.asqa.gov.au/sites/default/files/asqas_su
bmission_to_nvr_act_review.pdf?v=1522272883>

Australian Skills Quality Authority, 'National Vocational
Education and Training Regulator Fees and Charges for
Registration of Training Organisations, Accreditation of Courses
and Associated Services 2017-18 Consultation DRAFT'
(online at 24 June 2019)
<https://www.asqa.gov.au/file/8046/download?token
=qSqaouUX>

Australian Skills Quality Authority, 'Notice of Decision to
Cancel NVR Act Registration' template (no version
number, date).

Australian Skills Quality Authority, 'Regulatory Risk
Framework' (Report, April 2016)
<https://www.asqa.gov.au/sites/default/files/ASQA_
Regulatory_Risk_Framework.pdf?v=1508135481>

Australian Skills Quality Authority, 'Regulatory Strategy
2018-20' (Report)

LEGAL DECISION-MAKING UNDER THE
NATIONAL VOCATIONAL EDUCATION AND
TRAINING REGULATOR ACT 2011 (CTH): AN
INVESTIGATION INTO ACCESS TO MERITS
REVIEW

<https://www.asqa.gov.au/sites/default/files/asqa_reg
ulatory_strategy_2018-20.pdf?v=1540254512>

Carol Ey, 'The Vocational Education and Training
Sector: A Quick Guide' (Research Paper, Parliamentary
Library, Parliament of Australia, 19 November 2018)

Council of Australian Governments, *Council of Australian
Governments' Meeting Communiqué*, (February 2009)

Department of Education and Training (DET) 'Jobs
supported by international students studying in
Australia' (Research Snapshots, 2017)
<https://internationaleducation.gov.au/research/resear
ch-snapshots/pages/default.aspx>

Department of Education and Training (DET) 'Jobs
supported by international students studying in
Australia' (Research Snapshots, March 2019)
<https://internationaleducation.gov.au/research/Resear
ch-
Snapshots/Documents/RS_Job%20supported%202018.

LEGAL DECISION-MAKING UNDER THE
NATIONAL VOCATIONAL EDUCATION AND
TRAINING REGULATOR ACT 2011 (CTH): AN
INVESTIGATION INTO ACCESS TO MERITS
REVIEW

pdf>

Joint Standing Committee on Migration, Parliament of Australia, *Report of the Inquiry into Efficacy of Current Regulation of Australian Migration and Education Agents* (February 2019) <https://www.aph.gov.au/Parliamentary_Business/Committees/Joint/Migration/Migrationagentregulatio/Report>

Letter from Benn Gramola to Name Withheld, 11 April 2018, professional correspondence held on client's file - RTO Doctor

Letter from Benn Gramola to Name Withheld, 11 August 2017, professional correspondence held on client's file - RTO Doctor

Letter from Benn Gramola to Name Withheld, 15 January 2019, professional correspondence held on client's file - RTO Doctor

LEGAL DECISION-MAKING UNDER THE
NATIONAL VOCATIONAL EDUCATION AND
TRAINING REGULATOR ACT 2011 (CTH): AN
INVESTIGATION INTO ACCESS TO MERITS
REVIEW

Letter from Benn Gramola to Name Withheld, 22 November 2018, professional correspondence held on client's file - RTO Doctor

Letter from Benn Gramola to Name Withheld, 23 January 2019, professional correspondence held on client's file - RTO Doctor

Letter from Benn Gramola to Name Withheld, 29 March 2019, professional correspondence held on client's file - RTO Doctor

Letter from Benn Gramola to Name Withheld, 29 May 2019

Letter from Benn Gramola to Name Withheld, 29 May 2019, professional correspondence held on client's file - RTO Doctor

Letter from Benn Gramola to Name Withheld, 30 August 2017; professional correspondence held on client's file - RTO Doctor

LEGAL DECISION-MAKING UNDER THE
NATIONAL VOCATIONAL EDUCATION AND
TRAINING REGULATOR ACT 2011 (CTH): AN
INVESTIGATION INTO ACCESS TO MERITS
REVIEW

Tertiary Education   Standards Agency, '*What Approach to Quality Assurance and Regulation*' (Web Page) <https://www.teqsa.gov.au/what-we-do>

Tertiary Education   Standards Agency, '*What Approach to Quality Assurance and Regulation*' (Web Page) <https://www.teqsa.gov.au/what-we-do>

The Hon. Simon Birmingham 'Labour Blocks the Truth on TAFESA', Senator Birmingham (Web Page, 1 March 2018) <https://www.senatorbirmingham.com.au/labor-blocks-the-truth-on-tafe-sa/>

Tim Dodd, 'Regulator Denies Ghost College Claims', *The Australian* (online, 25 July 2019) 5 < https://www.theaustralian.com.au/higher-education/regulator-denies-ghost-college-claims/news-story/38b7c6e9ed9d426743fe37e6374d0499>

LEGAL DECISION-MAKING UNDER THE NATIONAL VOCATIONAL EDUCATION AND TRAINING REGULATOR ACT 2011 (CTH): AN INVESTIGATION INTO ACCESS TO MERITS REVIEW

Annexure A

Glossary of Terms

Auditor

Means a person who conducts an audit or compliance audit on behalf of the VET Regulator.
Standards for VET Regulators 2015 (Cth) Glossary

Foundation Program

Foundation Programs for international students are nationally recognised courses that equip these students with the skills and capabilities to seek entry into higher education programs in Australia. They provide an academic entry pathway to first year undergraduate study or its equivalent.
Foundation Program Standards, Preamble

ELICOS

For the purposes of the ELICOS Standards, an ELICOS course is a course of education or training that is:

- solely or predominantly of English language instruction; and

LEGAL DECISION-MAKING UNDER THE NATIONAL VOCATIONAL EDUCATION AND TRAINING REGULATOR ACT 2011 (CTH): AN INVESTIGATION INTO ACCESS TO MERITS REVIEW

- provided, or intended to be provided, to an overseas student as defined in section 5 of the ESOS Act.

Courses which <u>do not</u> fall within the definition of 'ELICOS' include, but are not limited to:

- English language programs provided exclusively to non-student visa holders;
- English as an additional language programs or support services provided within the school sector as part of a school curriculum; and
- Foundation Programs.

ELICOS Standards 2018, Introduction, Definition

LEGAL DECISION-MAKING UNDER THE NATIONAL VOCATIONAL EDUCATION AND TRAINING REGULATOR ACT 2011 (CTH): AN INVESTIGATION INTO ACCESS TO MERITS REVIEW

Special Codes

All of your special codes are listed below as a way of saying thank you for purchasing this book and giving us the opportunity to provide you with a professional development opportunity.

To access your special codes, follow the link to the RTO Doctor website https://rtodoctor.com.au/contact/

Type in your access code (limit of one per purchase).

Item	Discount	Code
Preliminary Consultation (up to 1 hour)	10%	CONSULT
Mentoring Program	10%	MENTOR
Comprehensive Risk Management Audit	10%	RISK

LEGAL DECISION-MAKING UNDER THE NATIONAL VOCATIONAL EDUCATION AND TRAINING REGULATOR ACT 2011 (CTH): AN INVESTIGATION INTO ACCESS TO MERITS REVIEW

Author Profile

Raelene is the Founding Director of RTO Doctor, a company in Australia specialising in sanction management and response, forensic auditing, specialist compliance management and supporting clients through complex appeals at the Australian Administrative Appeals Tribunal.

Raelene is currently completing a Bachelor of Laws (Graduate Entry) in the Faculty of Law at Murdoch University in Perth, Western Australia. She also holds qualifications in areas including Migration Law, Education, Quality Auditing, Training and Assessment, Adolescent Health and Welfare.

This book began as an academic paper for a required unit of study, LLB381 Supervised Legal Project. It has

LEGAL DECISION-MAKING UNDER THE NATIONAL VOCATIONAL EDUCATION AND TRAINING REGULATOR ACT 2011 (CTH): AN INVESTIGATION INTO ACCESS TO MERITS REVIEW

been slightly amended to include further commentary and explanation of some areas that needed further clarification but due to the word count required by the academic requirements of the unit, had to be removed. These sections have now been added to provide a better understanding and further clarification of some areas.

Having spent over 20 years in the education and training industry in many roles, Raelene has had the privilege of working with a range of experts in the Schools, VET, ELICOS & Higher Education sectors as a Consultant, various roles as a private provider and as a Regulator in International and Higher Education. It is this intricate integration of experience from every participant in the learning journey that allows Raelene to provide such sophisticated insight into a complex area of regulation.

LEGAL DECISION-MAKING UNDER THE NATIONAL VOCATIONAL EDUCATION AND TRAINING REGULATOR ACT 2011 (CTH): AN INVESTIGATION INTO ACCESS TO MERITS REVIEW

Raelene's experience can be traced back to her school days where, as a gifted student, she spent many hours outside of school mentoring her friends who were struggling to get through school in areas including English, French, Biology, Social Studies and Legal Studies. In 1989, Raelene started working as a Tutor in France teaching English as a Second Language & Remedial French to local French College students. In Tahiti, Raelene continued this work with the local Polynesians and French citizens on the island. As a qualified Secondary School Teacher & Adult Trainer, Raelene spent several years working in Prison Education (both adult & juvenile justice centres) and with marginalised young people in the Western Suburbs of Melbourne, Victoria (Australia). Raelene has worked with people from all different backgrounds including Non English Speaking Backgrounds (NESB), Homeless, people with substance abuse & mental health concerns,

234

LEGAL DECISION-MAKING UNDER THE
NATIONAL VOCATIONAL EDUCATION AND
TRAINING REGULATOR ACT 2011 (CTH): AN
INVESTIGATION INTO ACCESS TO MERITS
REVIEW

people with disabilities, international students and all the
way through to corporate clients.

Raelene is well respected by industry and regulators at
both State & Commonwealth level. Having been an
integral part of the National Re-Registration of all
CRICOS Providers across Australia in 2009 – 2010,
Raelene has been involved in many areas that traditional
Consultants rarely get to focus on and developed
relationships with key representatives of regulatory
agencies and industry bodies, strengthening an already
Remedial French to local French College students. In
Tahiti, Raelene continued this work with the local
Polynesians and French citizens on the island. As a
qualified Secondary School Teacher & Adult Trainer,
Raelene spent several years working in Prison Education
(both adult & juvenile justice centres) and with
marginalised young people in the Western Suburbs of

LEGAL DECISION-MAKING UNDER THE NATIONAL VOCATIONAL EDUCATION AND TRAINING REGULATOR ACT 2011 (CTH): AN INVESTIGATION INTO ACCESS TO MERITS REVIEW

Melbourne, Victoria (Australia). Raelene has worked with people from all different backgrounds including Non English Speaking Backgrounds (NESB), Homeless, people with substance abuse & mental health concerns, people with disabilities, international students and all the way through to corporate clients.

Raelene is well respected by industry and regulators at both State & Commonwealth level. Having been an integral part of the National Re-Registration of all CRICOS Providers across Australia in 2009 – 2010, Raelene has been involved in many areas that traditional Consultants rarely get to focus on and developed relationships with key representatives of regulatory agencies and industry bodies, rengthening an already strong network. She continues to be highly sought after by recruitment companies for high profile roles in training & professional development for large national &

LEGAL DECISION-MAKING UNDER THE NATIONAL VOCATIONAL EDUCATION AND TRAINING REGULATOR ACT 2011 (CTH): AN INVESTIGATION INTO ACCESS TO MERITS REVIEW

global companies and is consulted regularly by knowledge brokers around the world. Raelene has an unblemished success rate in complex sanction management and an impeccable audit history; she is highly sought after by leaders in international education around the globe.

www.ingramcontent.com/pod-product-compliance
Lightning Source LLC
Chambersburg PA
CBHW031837170526
45157CB00001B/331